Urban

Gardening

Building Your Own Herbal
Apothecary by Herb Gardening in
Your Home

*(Making Use of Cramped Spaces and Growing
Your Own Food for a Sustainable Living)*

Michael Parker

Published By **John Kembrey**

Michael Parker

Urban Gardening: Building Your Own Herbal Apothecary by Herb Gardening in Your Home (Making Use of Cramped Spaces and Growing Your Own Food for a Sustainable Living)

ISBN 978-1-998901-83-8

No part of this guidbook shall be reproduced in any form without permission in writing from the publisher except in the case of brief quotations embodied in critical articles or reviews.

Legal & Disclaimer

The information contained in this book is not designed to replace or take the place of any form of medicine or professional medical advice. The information in this book has been provided for educational & entertainment purposes only.

The information contained in this book has been compiled from sources deemed reliable, and it is accurate to the best of the Author's knowledge; however, the Author cannot guarantee its accuracy and validity and cannot be held liable for any errors or omissions. Changes are periodically made to this book. You must consult your doctor or get professional medical advice before using any of the suggested remedies, techniques, or information in this book.

Table of Contents

Chapter 1: Sustainable Living And Urban Gardening One Zero One

You can be wondering what sustainable residing is. Well, this is approximately being environmentally, socially, and economically accountable. It is set making aware and informed choices in each issue of your existence. This is to enhance your terrific of existence and hold what's left of this planet for future generations.

It isn't that dwelling sustainably manner which you are aware about the effect of your choices. Yes, it is a way of existence choice, however trade does not occur in a day. It is an experiential and ongoing gadget of gaining knowledge of and growing preexisting and new values.

Some of the questions that you want to ask yourself - Is there a need that permits you to trade your way of dwelling? Are there higher techniques you may enhance your desire-making tactics? Do products you devour have better options? Is there a need so that you can take a wreck from what you do robotically? What may want to you do at the identical time as you take a ruin from paintings?

Let's pause for a minute and answer the ones questions: Do you hold in thoughts what you possibly did within the last few days? Or the matters you obtain? How about the humans you talked to? Can you appearance five years into the destiny and recognize precisely in which you need to be? Have you reached in which you would like to be? If you responded NO to any of these questions, then you definitely truly've were given a solution as to why you need a exchange, a clean outlook in existence, or get a modern-day mind-set.

Today, we characteristic on autopilot; we do now not even understand what we are doing. We are so manipulated through using industrial merchandise that we do not even recognise it. Did that average households have over ten hundreds of fabric of their possessions in the US by myself? And that forty three% of households spend more than they earn. In the one year 2013, Americans have consumed over 154,000 kilos of Starbucks espresso; agree with the extensive style of Starbucks cups thrown with this cost of purchases.

Furthermore, we are overloaded through duties and responsibilities; it's far like we're digging our graves with regrets and frustrations. We have stopped noticing the subjects which is probably taking region proper in the front humans. It's time that is finished. Nobody desires to stay a lifestyles complete of regrets, and studies have proven that we remorse greater at the matters that we did not do than the matters we did. If you listing down the five matters that you price the most right now, you would possibly understand that you haven't finished a few trouble to reveal your values, and you may surprise if you price the ones in any respect. By residing a sustainable life, you cast off a majority of those extras and paintings on what's genuinely critical. Spend more time

3

together along with your family, take a look at what's to your ebook list, meet new friends, acquire research and recollections, plant your garden, and make your life profitable.

There are many methods to begin living sustainably. One of the most well-known, probably the most useful, and exceptional strategies to get you going in the direction of a higher you is through

Urban Gardening.

Nowadays, the town-lifestyles, sky-rise infrastructures, stores, and production corporations have become more awesome within the rural areas and turning into more invasive to our mountains and almost every available land. The stated "traits" generally goes with the reducing down of timber, blocking off the river paths, drying up the seas, producing more pollution, and intensifying climate exchange. Environmental activists and concerned residents initiated a Movement geared towards developing city community gardens. This is to make sure that people come collectively to expand meals vegetation with the intention to assist them meet their dreams for healthy food manufacturing.

Historically, metropolis gardening started out out as "allotment gardens" in Germany whilst food shortages and poverty have been rampant. Then, this software program boomed at a few degree inside the worldwide wars wherein survivors tilled "victory gardens" no longer first-rate to appease the want for meals but also for peaceful social interactions.

In the nineteenth century, in the course of World War I even as the then American president, Woodrow Wilson, ordered that every empty land be used for food production. Food shortages have been rampant, and they not had sufficient meals assets for his or her soldiers and other personnel. Within two many years, five million land plots have been cultivated, and 500 million pounds of meals were produced. This paved the way to the introduction of the National Victory Garden Program, from which such programs were organized to have agricultural gardens inside towns.

Poverty and emotional turmoil are just of the natural outcomes of warfare. However, thru using collecting the community to cultivate their land, sow herbs, culmination, and veggies; and harvest them collectively. Urban gardening has furnished an street to benefit a number of their identity, enjoy of belongingness, and independence. Throughout information, particularly at some stage in the bottom factors of humanity, planting introduced the network together and stored people alive.

These historic occasions formed the urban gardening movement that it's far in recent times. Nowadays, metropolis agriculture is covered into numerous cities' plans and packages to integrate recommendations geared closer to building sustainable agencies.

Not high-quality did the town agriculture motion infiltrate public suggestions, but it moreover permeated the non-public quarter thru smaller town gardens. Food manufacturing has become a shared responsibility, dividing the greater huge troubles of food shortages and environmental damages. For all and sundry who engages in metropolis gardening and begins generating their non-public meals, the greater human beings are fed and the lighter the weight to mom earth. With the growing wide kind of human beings becoming aware of this answer, we won't need to deal with troubles of terrible existence, famine, malnutrition, and climate trade, amongst others.

Bill Gates, one of the global's richest guys, declared that "making an investment in agriculture, brings one of the maximum returns you could ever have." True to his word, it's miles actually possible to feed the sector if handiest we're capable of decide out a way to try this without depleting our herbal property. By the give up of this ebook, you could discover ways to feed yourself and a manner to stay a healthful manner of life.

Chapter 2: How Urban Gardening Will Amp Up Your Life

To many people, flora and gardening certainly have an impact on their lives, however as a bargain as what amount? Well, essentially, in almost every problem of their lives, flowers and gardening make it higher.

In this financial disaster, you can studies some studies and scientific strategies on how vegetation have improved our way of life. Hopefully, this can encourage you to pursue city gardening and effect awesome people to take on the addiction as well.

Better Performance

Studies have shown that plants have a natural calming impact that permits cognizance and lets in decorate reminiscence. In a specific observe, electrodes have been connected to the contributors' heads to reveal mind interest, physiological signs and symptoms which encompass coronary heart expenses, sweating, and pulse costs. The effects showed that once the people touched a plant, the highbrow and physiological symptoms of stress and anxiety drastically reduced. Participants have grow to be calmer and additional aware.

In a few specific have a look at, two busy offices had been as compared. One had plant foliage, and the opposite did now not have any greeneries in any respect. Interestingly, there has been lesser noise within the office with flowers compared to the opportunity with out greeneries. People then worked higher and were greater centered on paintings, ensuing in better productiveness. In the towns nowadays, many offices or maybe some residences are windowless. Thus, the ones enclosed regions behavior plenty noise and distraction without a outlet, vegetation have been able to lower those problems. Another beneficial give up quit result will be that place of work people grow to be plenty less irritable and turn out to be extra harmonious in running with extraordinary people.

According to research, there can be proof that demonstrates nature or the presence of vegetation improves overall performance. In one have a take a look at, individuals who worked in an environmental condition showed 20% reminiscence improvement, usual standard performance, and accuracy in a given assignment than the members who were positioned inside the not unusual place of job setting.

Plants can stimulate your mind and the senses, which lets in preserve up the strength and the mind ability at top-notch. For humans who've a busy art work existence, difficulties concentrating and recalling matters, it could be tough to get proper of access to inexperienced areas suitable for art work. One element that you want to word is that parks are not generally appropriate running environments. Therefore, the fantastic alternative is probably to create your lawn and attain all the highbrow, physical, and intellectual advantages that plants can offer.

Leaving a Legacy

If we do now not exchange our procedures right now, the possibilities are that our children and grandchildren will not be capable of enjoy the satisfactory of nature is excessive. Trees may additionally not exist in cities, and weather alternate will hold to turn out to be one of the most important environmental troubles worldwide.

By studying a manner to lawn at home, we are also training the children on a way to stay to tell the tale in the destiny. This isn't always some thing that they could examine in the test room; planting is experiential and emotional. Through farming, you're elevating a infant with superior interest, a infant who's aware, and a toddler who's grateful for the simple subjects in existence.

This is every other cause humans ought to constantly marketing and advertising marketing marketing campaign to hold and assemble inexperienced areas, public botanical gardens, or vegetable patches in the community. Hence, fostering obligation amongst citizens and children. With the short acceleration of virtual conversation, humans are slowly disregarding personal connections, but those locations can help bring the community together.

Within the confines of your property, gardening projects provide an street for the circle of relatives to get together and spend extra extraordinary time. For example, whilst celebrating an success, a own family can also select out to plant a seed together as a photograph of figuring out a aim. They can then watch that plant expand in remembrance in their past achievements.

Plants are our Source of Happiness

It is scientifically tested that flora want to supply pleasure, reduce stress and signs and symptoms and signs of despair, further to increase tremendous electricity. Flowers, especially, are recognized to beautify one's temper right away. They should make you revel in snug, satisfied, and solid.

Evolutionarily, vegetation and flowers were humanity's allies. They supplied us with food, refuge, protection from predators, and vegetation symbolize that give up end result are quick to appear and offer vitamins for the community. So, no matter the manner you are saying that you do not like flora or anticipate that it's far too girly or cheesy, we're actually willing to love flora.

Flowers make you have a better outlook on existence, and it's far truely one of these naturally stunning topics in the global without all of the pretensions and alterations. So, if you want to make someone happy (lover, pal, or member of the family), flowers are one of the quality presents to present.

However, doing that might price you extensively as some flower types are in particular costly. The solution? Plant your non-public vegetation! Freshly picked flowers you broaden your self show lots of strive, sincerity, and a personal contact. Giving plant life this way is assured to be better favored than preserve-offered ones.

Health and Wellness

Did you already know that the pharmaceutical agency is one of the richest and fastest-developing sectors in the international? The hassle is that those corporations regularly sell horrible ingesting conduct, sedentary life-style, stress, and masses of more sickness-causing factors. This explains why increasingly more people go through persistent degenerative sicknesses at a very more youthful age, which make these pharmaceutical groups richer.

It is certainly a 3-way hassle with a honest answer.

Unhealthy Diet

The meals we eat nowadays is each full of awful cholesterol or whole of unnatural chemical substances or each. Even on the equal time as groups label their products as "natural," this isn't always an guarantee which you are consuming healthful substances. You want to recognize that the usage of the time period "herbal" on their labels can be a marketing and advertising and advertising scheme geared toward deceiving clients into buying their products.

If you develop your meals organically, you recognize what is going into your frame, and also you understand which you're consuming healthful. Understandably, you can not increase all meals factors to your personal. Therefore, you may pick out to buy licensed herbal meals, that is particularly greater high priced than industrially produced gadgets. The right information is which you get to lessen down on costs with the aid of developing some of them for your garden.

Sedentary Lifestyle

More specially, a sedentary way of lifestyles in that you've were given near no longer some thing in phrases of workout or every different bodily activity. Around 60% of the arena's population spends an average of 6 to 7 hours sitting down, and about 35% of them spend a mean of 4 hours mendacity down at the equal time as searching television or spending hundreds time browsing the net at the computer or cell device.

United Kingdom's National Health Service (NHS) related sitting an excessive amount of or sedentary way of lifestyles to numerous health issues together with weight issues, excessive blood stress, kind II diabetes, powerful sorts of most cancers, and early demise. Gardening can help lessen the time you spend sitting down every day due to the fact you are the use of it in looking after your flowers. Even thirty mins of physical exercise from gardening each day is already a first-rate improvement as compared to having infinite hours of sitting or lying down and doing not anything. This way, your frame turns into more healthy and you furthermore come to be extra green.

Outside Health Risk Factors

Pollution, noise, and congestion are actually three matters outdoor of our manage but they may manipulate our temper and strain tiers. They weaken the body's immune machine, making you an smooth cause for pathogens and ailments. We already understand how flora can mediate all of these outdoor impacts. But you want to comprehend that the act of gardening is a scientifically demonstrated way to lessen the stresses of lifestyles.

With gardening, you may beautify your self-reliance, revel in extra finished, and be capable of facilitate social interactions with others. When you've got have been given all that taking place, you'll be masses an awful lot less bothered via what is going on outdoor; you emerge as greater conscious of what is great and get rid of the distractions.

Natural Pain-Reliever

Plants do not pleasant offer long-lasting effects on our nicely-being, however they've immediately consequences as well. In a famous take a look at, medical institution sufferers who underwent an operation have been sent to two unique recovery rooms. The first one had vegetation in it, at the same time as the second became only a silly antique health center room.

As expected, the affected man or woman in the plant room stated feeling a good buy less ache than the affected person in the distinct room. Moreover, the primary affected individual recovered faster than the second one affected character. Plants also are applied in most most cancers and geriatric facilities to assist sufferers address their bodily and emotional treatments.

Through horticulture therapy, patients recovered drastically faster than common because of the reality they have been allowed to plant and deal with them. Similarly, if you have your very own garden, you may have masses much less time delivering your remedy cupboard for aspirin or every different medicine for that bear in mind.

Mental Health

If you have got were given a family member, a friend, or all people who is probably affected by highbrow issues, you could recommend that they take in gardening. Gardening is frequently used as experiential treatment, specially for human beings with depression, tension, and particular intellectual issues. It promotes self-reliance and can help improve conceitedness which can bring about an improvement on their notion approximately positive matters including themselves.

People who went via trauma are also advocated to immerse themselves in nature. It changed into additionally decided that kids with interest deficit issues cope higher with plant life around them or in a placing this is surrounded with nature.

Beauty in a Natural Scenery

People are regularly attracted to herbal perspectives and symmetries, and having flora in or round your home will increase its enchantment. A better degree of perceived beauty additionally will increase the perceived superb of existence.

Having a herbal foliage in your own home makes it look higher and greater steeply-priced than it definitely is. This furthermore undoubtedly affects the network due to the fact your house might be a version for making the community look aesthetically captivating.

Life-Saver and Giver

No take into account how we overlook our environment, it's far an easy fact that we can not stay without flora. The international can't exist without plant life. Plants provide us with oxygen, easy air, food, and nutrients. Not to mention, flora protect us from calamities. Floods occur because of the truth we do no longer have sufficient timber and soil anymore to take inside the water from the rains.

Now that we have were given understood and desired the placement of vegetation in our lives, it's time that we display our appreciation with the beneficial resource of planting and preserving them. The nice way to do that is thru growing our city gardens just so we are able to have a non-save you supply of food, extra healthy lifestyle, and wholesome environment as properly. Read on via the following financial ruin to get your self started out on making your very very own metropolis garden.

Chapter 3: Self And House Preparations For Making Your Own Urban Garden

A lawn with small plants is pretty like having a new infant popping out of the ground. The birthing approach and the traumatic techniques may moreover fluctuate, but infants and flora each want masses of TLC and self-discipline.

Some of you can feel threatened thru this, mainly as it requires an excessive amount of dedication than you initially concept about. However, you do now not ought to fear because it does now not remaining all the time. Just like any other offspring, they all increase and go out of the nest. However, with flora, it takes a quick time for them to mature (enough a good way to go away them on my own).

Now, let us get into planting!

First, you could want a cup of willpower. As cited earlier than, gardening takes time and severa difficult art work however the entire element are worthwhile due to the truth you could experience a feel of fulfillment in the end. Gardening isn't quite an lousy lot planting the seeds and leaving them there; you moreover mght need to spend time in looking after them as they keep growing relying on the plant range and the season.

It is an prolonged manner that includes weeding, watering, and cleansing, in addition to removing insects and bugs. These are simply some of the stuff which you need to do. Yes, those are definitely small sacrifices that you have to make as compared to the prolonged listing of benefits which can be diagnosed in the preceding financial disaster about how plants will trade your life for the higher.

You may have a look at this upkeep section and extra difficult art work as your new exercising regime. Because this is the undertaking of metropolis gardening: selling health in each problem of your life.

Remove that photograph of flawlessly manicured gardens you note in magazines and advertisements due to the fact town gardening may require greater creativity than that. The available place and the kind of surroundings you live in play a large characteristic in identifying the manner to harness all your creativity and resourcefulness. This ensures that you create a completely conducive environment on your flowers to flourish.

If you go searching your location, you could get a hint discouraged wondering that flowers couldn't match or develop there, but you are wrong. Plants are strong creatures that, collectively with your assist, may also want to stand through any surroundings.

Look round your region all over again and consider each to be had area as a ability garden. To make deciding on flowers and put together containers less complicated, strive pre-conceptualizing in which you can placed up your garden.

Look via each corner and cranny; if you've identified a vicinity in which you want to put in your plant life, take the vital measurements for that. Taking the size ought to provide you with a sensible image of your lawn, making your existence less complex at the same time as you begin installing the boxes, and selecting the flora' right length.

Your garden need to have ok get admission to to daylight, proper air flow, and water for irrigation. Weeding want to be carried out in your selected place without continually having to worry approximately making a mess.

Once the entirety has been worked out and also you keep in mind which you are ready for a exchange in your manner of life, then take a look at on to start installing your first town garden. The next chapters will help you recognize the specific sorts of materials you could recycle for growing your flora. You can also moreover even have an belief at the manner to set them up to suit your lanai, rooftop, balcony, or out of doors further to deciding on the right vegetation with a cause to suit your area and needs.

Chapter 4: Right Space, Right Place To Put Your Plants In

When you live in an city putting, having huge open areas, like a outdoor or a garden, is a luxurious that now not many can find the money for. If you're one of these who have very confined region, you could have to utilize numerous bins to increase your flowers. Containers assist you to maximize the little region which you have and preserve your garden organized.

So, this financial ruin will introduce you to severa varieties of boxes that you can use to increase your vegetation in. These substances must both be keep-supplied or in case you are maintaining with the sustainable way of life that you have started out, you can use containers which is probably fabricated from recycled materials. You also can look at numerous DIY thoughts on the way to be supplied here so you can decorate your garden and make it your private fashion.

These are the boxes at the manner for use on this bankruptcy, on the aspect of the instructions on a manner to use, location, and decorate them:

- Pots

- Raised beds

- Hanging baskets

- Other recyclable materials

Pots

They are the maximum easy and trendy packing containers that you could discover anywhere. They have a large form of sizes, materials used, and colors.

Some of the equal antique pots we understand are the terra cotta pot, water-proof glazed pots, wood pots, and plastic pots. The latest pottery enhancements are made of artificial materials, which includes: resin, fiberglass, propylene, or even cloth pots.

If you do no longer have any of those pots, you could choose out out to use an antique bucket, basket, or watering can. After all, they look like pots anyway; drill a few holes at the bottom to make sure you've got right drainage in your vegetation.

To make the proper desire on sure sorts of pots that you may use, maintain in mind those 3 subjects: weight, porosity, and drainage.

If you live in a cramped space, it's miles critical to move things fast to get them out of the manner or create more location. Thus, it is essential to choose the materials that offer the most awesome mobility. None of the big clay and wood pots is the remarkable opportunity for you. This is due to the reality most of them are heavy and need to component within the soil's weight and the plant itself. So, select smaller pots, in particular because you're although beginning. If needed you could switch them to a bigger pot at later time.

The distinct component is porosity, it is the pot's belongings to permit air to flow into inside the plant's root gadget. This is important due to the fact oxygen is important in the plant's photosynthesis, it's far vital for it to undergo plant life and end end result.

Porosity additionally gives the plant a threat to eliminate extra water and cooling down the soil. The greater porous the sector, the extra successfully the soil will dry out, so you will need to water the plants extra often. Pots made from terra cotta, peat, and timber are a few which have the maximum porosity.

Last however now not least is drainage. No do not forget what type of cloth you operate, containers need to continuously have a right water drainage, most in all likelihood within the form of holes. Glazed pots and fiberglass pots are water-proof, which means that they may ultimate longer considering the fact that they'll be proof closer to harm thru moisture.

Be careful whilst purchasing cheap plastic pots due to the fact they speedy come to be brittle while exposed to intense climate situations. Otherwise, you can come to be searching for new ones every on occasion.

There isn't any need to buy new pots all of the time; you could reuse even the broken boxes if you have them. You can location some of the smaller vegetation in there and use the broken portions to dam the soil from overflowing. You also can beautify it with vintage toys in case you want to create a smooth landscape layout from a single broken pot.

To save on area, you could dedicate a massive pot in that you plant your rosemary, parsley, basil, and green onions alongside the rim of the massive pot. These herbs may be reduce or trimmed for harvesting effortlessly, so that you might probable not should fear about the flowers overflowing the pot due to the reality you may rapid pick out out them out. You can also contain twine meshes inside the middle or round your area to prepare for larger fruit plant life and some vines.

The handiest manner to beautify a pot is to coloration it. Choose a climate-resistant paint, something natural, or one crafted from non-toxic materials to make certain that the flora do not get risky chemical substances in them.

Pros: Highly to be had inside the marketplace, clean to installation, is available in unique paperwork and sizes.

Cons: Difficult to customise and limited as regards to placement, they will be fragile, and they will be in particular greater bulky.

Top spot to your pots: For the small flowers in miniature pots, you may spread them round your house. On the edge of your home windows and tables, you may hang your flowering plant life. For the bigger pots, you can location them beside your door, each outside or inner, this is, after confirming the actual top, you can finally emerge as. So, for large plants, it might be quality to area them out of doors if you have any area or in any of the empty corners of the room. You can keep close some of the smaller pots throughout the big pot or actually set up the small ones around the big one.

Raised Beds

Raised beds are frequently made from timber or lumber. They are widely available in the marketplace. You can choose out to shop for a hard and fast on-line or with the useful resource of going into brick-and-mortar lawn stores. Alternatively, you can assemble your raised mattress using vintage refurbished wood or lumber slats you can have round in your junk hold.

Raised beds are satisfactory for city gardening due to the significance of pollutants gift within the soil and the reality that there may be no soil round you sufficient for planting. The accurate element about raised beds is that they are outstanding area savers. They may additionally appearance large and intimidating, however they will be able to hold masses of vegetation in only one area of your vicinity. You also can landscape it with the aid of the use of having stacked raised beds, arranging your flowers relying on boom length and yield.

They additionally provide a valid drainage tool, and it lets in for deep rooting for your flowers. If your plant life' root growth is stunted, it could propose that your vegetation could now not bear any end end result. Wooden raised beds are weather or season-proof due to the fact the soil is not touching the ground; you'll have more manipulate close to the soil temperature. Lastly, raised beds can defend your plants from risky worms and insects.

If you have got determined to make your very very own raised mattress, you'll need the subsequent substances:

Lumber or wood: 2" x 4" or 6" or 8" planks, depending on how long you want it to be. More high priced wood has herbal oils that would prevent it from rotting. Pressure-tested wooden is secure as it is licensed to be stable for planting. Two-inch thick forests are first-class for farming because they may last longer closer to wet and extraordinary damaging conditions.

-    Stakes: need to be about three feet lengthy, 1 to two inches in diameter, and at the least four portions. These are essential because of the truth the ones are what decorate the timber bed.

- Hammers

- Nails or screws

- Leveling tool

So, the steps required for building a pallet of any period are the following:

To make the edges, area planks of timber factor with the aid of side and be part of them with a smaller piece of wooden at each ends. Using the equal measurements, do this for the opposite component. The sizeable period for a timber raised mattress is four toes, and the depth need to be no shorter than 12 inches deep for conducive root boom.

Given which you possibly notable have a small area spherical your home to location your flowers, it'd be better to make the planter a bit narrower. So, for the 2 closing components, stack the woods with the identical height measurements due to the reality the primary ones, however make the length shorter this time.

Assemble the four portions with nails or screws to form a rectangle or rectangular.

You may additionally moreover now vicinity extra planks of wooden in the course of the corners to make the floor mattress.

Make fantastic to head away small gaps for air glide and drainage.

DIY Idea: To create extra area, you may want to stack those containers collectively. There are approaches to try this. First, create a tall frame closer to a wall in which you could connect your organized-made containers with nails or screws. This is right for small bins, and you could set up the containers asymmetrically for layout functions.

Second, you can create a shelf with the packing containers. You will nevertheless want a frame, however your beds should be longer. If you do no longer have that plenty wall place to art work with, you could personalize the form of your field in step with the size of what available area you've got. You can also create a trellis spherical your frames to contain the vines and big flowers.

Pros: Customizable, have larger garage capability, gives accurate drainage and plant safety.

Cons: Vulnerable to rotting and weather situations, hard to region within the residence, hard to collect.

Top spot for raised beds: You can location the ones proper outdoor your backdoor, or you could placed them proper through manner of your window as a plant discipline; it might assist enhance your view.

Hanging Containers

You will experience placing containers in most instances due to the fact they will be customizable. You have the possibility to design them as you want, an interest that you could have interaction your youngsters at. This is a big location saver due to the truth at the same time as you won't have some of vicinity in your private home, you can generally appoint the headspace.

By hanging your boxes and flowers, you could additionally create a self-irrigating tool that helps with saving water. The substances you could use are recycled materials, and the rest are matters you could locate at your number one arts and crafts shop.

You ought to use the two maximum commonplace substances on your setting garden, and people are baskets and plastic bottles. For every substances, they need to be light-weight sufficient to grasp them and strong to maintain your flora.

For baskets, you need to make sure that they have holes for drainage. These are brilliant for flowering vegetation or aromatic herbs. Just consider coming domestic each day to a glowing-smelling domestic from the herbs and plant life you've got placing round. The most often used baskets are the plastic ones and the conventional cord baskets, which you can get out of your network gardening keep.

Empty plastic bottles are a lot more customizable than the hampers, and you could additionally contribute loads in terms of defensive the environment through decreasing trash. You may want to make individual putting bottles or have a wall-like form product of plastic bottles as plant packing containers. Plastic bottles are best suitable for small herbs and flowers; they'll be not recommended for massive flowers or shrubs.

You will want the subsequent substances:

- Plastic bottles (at least 1.5 liters every)

- Cutter/scissors

- Nylon string or fishing string

- Washers

- Art substances (colored pens and paints)

Steps on How to Hang Plastic Bottle Containers

Step 1

Place your bottle on a flat and empty desk or ground. If you want to have individual placing bottles, location your bottle proper thing up. But if you're going to stack them, region your bottle horizontally.

Step 2

With your cutter, reduce a rectangular hollow an inch from the bottle's neck as a great deal as the center of the body (for vertical bottles). For horizontal bottles, lessen a larger hole 2 inches below the bottle's neck as an awful lot as an inch from the bottom. The width have to be approximately 2 to three inches.

Step three

Poke small holes along the perimeters of the bottle in which the string will undergo. Also, poke some holes in the backside of the bottles for drainage.

Step four

Pull the string via the small holes you poked and tie them with the washing machine to save you them from moving or sliding. Leave 1 to two toes of location from the pinnacle of the string to the pinnacle of the bottle for placing. For stacking bottles, repeat steps 1 to a few for two more bottles and string them together.

Step five

Now, begin redecorating. You also can additionally ask your kids to coloration your bottles with any decorations you need. More famous decorations are lovely animal faces, especially for the vertical bottles. Or you could label every bottle decoratively with the name of your infant or with the plant's call to make it educational and smooth to end up aware about whilst harvesting.

Top spot for placing packing containers: The home windows and at your the the front door are the awesome bets on wherein you can place your setting containers. These bins are small sufficient that they don't look worrying and messy. Instead, they look very adorable and captivating. If you have got an uneventful wall in your home, do now not have the energy to attach an entire new wallpaper, or coins to shop for artwork or frames, you may layout your walls with those flowers alternatively.

Pros: Customizable, a laugh to create, easy and decorative, location saver.

Cons: Not conducive for larger flowers, and soil must fast dry out.

Other Recyclable Materials

Practically any subject big sufficient to maintain flora and deep enough to contain its roots may be used for town gardening. If you have got were given browsed thru the internet for a few DIY thoughts, you can have seen an entire lot of watering cans, antique bathtubs, tires, or jars.

For seedlings, you could use egg trays and jam jars to plant them. You can decorate your jars as favored the usage of decorative paper and ribbons. Then, line them up to your window sill. These seedlings additionally make a wonderful gift to offer your friends, own family, or colleagues who would like to start their very own town garden. You can region your younger vegetation in jars in case you're regardless of the truth that liberating up vicinity from your private home or if you think they will be not however prepared for too much publicity.

As for tires, be cautious with the use of in recent times synthetic ones because of the fact they encompass chemical substances that are not wholesome for the soil and your plant life. Old tires are beneficial particularly due to the fact they've got pretty some available space in case you need to get modern. You can use them to panorama particular plant species and create a small lawn within the tire.

While the antique chairs and tables is probably reused as shelving for your flowers, attempt collecting all of the scrap substances you have in your home or storage. Harnessing all of your creative juices and stepping into planting.

Chapter 5: Plants - From Pots To Plates

If you may live a sustainable lifestyles, then you definitely need to devour healthy additives and exercising a healthful lifestyle. This can also advocate which you need to broaden your very non-public food to eliminate all the harmful chemical compounds which might be commonly utilized by many meals production organizations that might take a toll on our lives.

Not most effective that, don't forget how a lot money and time you will shop with the useful resource of getting your meals source in your very very own house! The fact is that you may get to enjoy a sparkling garden salad that surely got here from your very personal outdoor; how cool is that?

The consolation and experience of success are unrivaled. This bankruptcy will assist you satisfy your gardening thoughts. But, first, you need to find out the fundamental herbs and veggies that you may plant in your garden. You furthermore need to apprehend the right care, quantity of yield, and the way to increase them.

Being a newbie, the number one herbs and veggies are the best flowers that you can increase for your lawn. As you analyze more approximately gardening and familiarize yourself with high-quality plant types, you can start planting plants and fruit timber, that are a chunk complex and more complicated to increase.

If you're shopping for seeds from a gardening keep for the primary time, you've got not anything to worry approximately because of the fact they have got labels and facts supplied for you. So, choose out the seedlings labeled with "small" or "specific for packing containers" or "miniatures" or "shrubs."

Unless you've got were given enough vicinity for it, you can pick out the "jumbos" or "medium" seedlings. And in case you are sticking with a healthy way of lifestyles, it'd be outstanding if you can seek out herbal or heirloom seedlings. They might cost a bit a bit greater, but you'll now not need a exquisite deal besides due to the truth your plants are gadgets that hold on giving, so one seedling would possibly pass a protracted manner.

Moreover, the superb manner to increase herbs and greens is to organization them in line with their season. Some plant life thrive with the bloodless at the same time as others wither with too much solar; and vice versa. It's essential to phrase what seasons tremendous flowers bloom so that you don't waste some time and resources in retaining them.

For heat season plant life, those plants need warmth soil to develop. The fine time to plant those is at the surrender of the wintry weather season and harvest at the end of spring or summer season – relying on the plant's increase charge. Before planting them, you may preserve them indoors or place them in non-porous bins, which includes plastic, to keep away from drying the soil out. The identical goes for cold season plants except in contrary seasonal order.

Hot Season Plants

Peppers

Peppers are one of the healthiest meals that we consume, in particular bell peppers. Scientifically, they may be referred to as Capsicum Annuum. These small and colourful vegetables are loaded with Vitamin C. This form of weight loss plan allows facilitate iron absorption and may provide you with antioxidants to combat in competition to the symptoms and symptoms of having vintage.

Peppers moreover burn a number of calories, and that they save you hypertension thru having nutrition B6 and magnesium. They additionally include lycopene, which offers them colour and offers us protection from maximum cancers cells. It is awesome how one small vegetable can provide you with hundreds vitamins, right? Well, it is immoderate time you made this veggie a part of your every day weight-reduction plan via having them round every day on your lawn.

Unlike cucumbers, peppers are slow-developing, so that you may additionally moreover want to incubate the seeds interior in the course of springtime or purchase seedlings for transplants then take them out in the summer season. Before you placed within the seed, insert a stick to your pot or decided on field. The stick should help preserve the plant upright, and it have to be about 3 to four toes tall. Or you can set up a body or trellis to maintain extra region.

If you selected small varieties of pepper, you is probably able to plant 2 to 3 seeds in a 14-inch subject. Fill your region along side your soil mix until about an inch from the rim. Dig approximately an inch to plant your seeds in, 5 at most to be thinned out later. Place the field wherein there can be direct daylight and water them regularly.

Fertilize your plants as quickly as every 2 to 3 weeks from planting. Use natural and water-soluble fertilizers as an lousy lot as feasible. Harvest the culmination of your hard work as quickly because the pepper has ripened. There are more than one varieties of peppers that you can use, from bell peppers to chili peppers. You can combine high-quality colored species in a single vicinity to make an appealing lawn.

Tomatoes

Tomatoes are flexible; they will be everywhere inside the food that we eat. They are in our pasta, pizza, condiments, salads, and soups. Tomatoes are one of the most harvested vegetables anywhere within the international. But if you pick out your sauces to be selfmade and not entire of chemical substances, it is superb to make your personal by way of developing your tomatoes.

This great vegetable consists of a phytochemical called lycopene, which allows enhance immunity and prevents the increase of cancer cells. They are excessive in antioxidants and nutrients to prevent strain and age-associated illnesses. Tomatoes additionally contain healthy acids to facilitate the breaking down of glucose to

49

transform into energy that is beneficial for diabetic sufferers.

Choline is likewise one in every of its vitamins this is chargeable for retaining our cells and muscle groups healthful. It is showed to encompass healthy omega-three acids that sell a wholesome coronary coronary heart. As if it couldn't get any better than this, tomatoes moreover comprise folic acid that prevents the producing of a wonderful mind chemical that is answerable for emotions of despair. Hence, not only do tomatoes keep us wholesome, however further they keep us happy and energized.

The quality way of growing tomatoes is to use massive pots. You can allocate as a minimum a rectangular foot of location for this plant; then, you can area a stick or trellis round it to contain the leaves from taking over extra space. You will need some aspect this is approximately 18 centimeters in top to residence the roots of the tomato plant.

If you've got access to it, location a small fiberglass screen at the lowest of your pot to save you the soil from draining along side your water. A saucer can even help in draining the water greater thoroughly; the ones generally encompass business pots.

Using plastic pots to increase the tomatoes ensures that they have get right of entry to to exact sufficient daylight within the path of the day. Otherwise, they'll grow massive, hindering your mobility.

Cucumbers

Cucumbers or scientifically called Cucumis Sativus, are one of the tremendously cultivated vegetation inside the worldwide. And why not? They have very low-calorie content material material, and they don't have any ldl cholesterol. They are pinnacle to your fitness because of the truth they consist of fiber that cleanses your colon and promotes healthful pores and skin.

Moreover, the ones greens are excessive in potassium, antioxidants, vitamins A, B, C, and K, reducing excessive blood pressure and facilitating bone increase. You can pick numerous sorts as nicely, like Northern Cucumber, Bush Pickle, and Lemon Cucumbers.

Cucumbers are higher grown in a raised mattress with a frame or trellis at some stage in the mattress as cucumbers develop in vines. If you're starting from seeds, make sure to attend for two weeks after the very last iciness frost to ensure that the soil is warmness sufficient for the seeds to germinate. If you're transplanting, make sure to maintain the seeds inside the residence underneath warmness mild bulbs.

When you plant them, dig a hollow in the soil approximately half of to an inch deep. Drop 5 to eight seeds inside the soil, this can boom your chance of achievement, but you may need to transfer a few in a while. Then, softly cowl the seeds with soil but do now not pat or squish the soil in region; it'll harm the seeds.

If you are transplanting, be very careful in handling the seedling. Make high-quality that the soil is tough sufficient in order not to harm the roots, after which plant them a foot other than every distinctive. Once you have got planted the seeds and seedlings, water your flowers regularly. Do now not oversaturate the pot or mattress; make certain that the water flows to the bottom and drops from the drainage holes.

Cucumbers require moist soil to expand. Stick your finger up on your knuckles to test the soil's moisture content material material cloth. If your fingertip comes out wet, it suggests that the soil's moisture levels are adequate. If it's miles dry, water slowly and frequently to ensure that the soil is absorbing it.

Add natural fertilizers as soon as each three-four weeks to assist keep the moisture and hold the plant healthful, it is endorsed to use water-soluble and natural fertilizers. Also, make certain to guard your cucumber from the wind, specifically at some point of springtime. It is satisfactory to location them closer to a wall or a fence. Neem oil is an powerful pesticide, and it is herbal, so it's far steady to use collectively along side your vegetables or herbs.

Cucumbers are a quick-growing vegetable, so assume some end result internal a few weeks, approximately 50 to 70 days. Harvest cucumbers whilst they despite the fact that look younger and inner small to medium duration. Cucumbers get bitter as they age.

Herbs

You can plant those glowing and fragrant herbs along facet your greens, or you may area them in a single field. These are very compact, and you can replant them via merely slicing a stem diagonally and sticking it to the soil, except for Rosemary and Tarragon.

The place need to be 8 to 10 inches deep, and you could have 2 to a few herbs in line with square inch.

The herbs below thrive in warm and dry conditions, so make certain that they're uncovered to sunlight hours, however maintain the soil moisturized, mainly with basil and stevia.

- Oregano

- Rosemary

- Sage

- Tarragon

- Thyme

- Marjoram

- Basil

- Stevia

Cold Season Plants

Cauliflower

This cute flower-like vegetable has been referred to as a superfood. And it's miles no wonder as it consists of dietary fiber, antioxidants, anti-inflammatory homes, vitamins and minerals, and phytochemicals that fight in the direction of maximum cancers, high blood pressure, and kidney issues.

This cruciferous vegetable need to be planted at the 2 to the three-month mark, this means that after the closing frost of the wintry weather season or on the quit of the overdue spring or summer season seasons. Cauliflowers require pots like that of the tomatoes, 12 inches deep and 12 inches in diameter. For bloodless season plant life, it is advanced to use transplants or seedlings.

Fill your subject with soil until an inch earlier than the rim. Make a hollow within the center sufficient to in shape a seedling's roots or a smaller one for seeds. If you have got got have been given seedlings, softly remove them from the nursery pots thru squeezing both aspects till the plant slides out. After which, use the alternative hand to vicinity the plant into the pot lightly. For seeds, location at maximum four seeds inside the hollow. Then, gently cover with soil and water to preserve it moisturized. Put in pH-balanced water-soluble fertilizer.

Place the field outside one month earlier than the wintry weather season and ensure that it's miles uncovered to daylight. You can place your pot for your balcony or a raised area for maximum coolness. Don't ever permit the soil to transport dry really.

Blanch your cauliflowers at the same time as its diameter reaches 2 to a few inches. You could be conscious that its shade green, but you can turn it white with the aid of protecting the pinnacle with its leaves tied together at the pinnacle. The advanced diameter for harvesting is 7 inches or round 3 to 4 months (for transplants).

Use a pointy knife to lessen under the pinnacle sufficient to include leaves in your harvest to achieve your cauliflower. Do not reuse the soil to put in one in all a type plants due to the fact you're setting future flora at higher threat of ailments.

This planting process is likewise applicable to specific cruciferous flowers, which include broccoli, cabbage, kale, Brussels sprout, and turnips.

Spinach

Probably every toddler hates spinach, and each figure who desires to maintain their toddler wholesome pressure-feed this to them. But, if you contain your youngsters in planting and harvesting this plant, it's far likely that there might be a whole lot much less resistance to ingesting this vegetable within the next meal. This is also Popeye's well-known deliver of superpower because clearly, when you have this on your weight loss plan, you may begin feeling as sturdy as Popeye.

This vegetable consists of iron, calcium, potassium, and phosphorous, which might be concerned in muscle and bone building. It moreover consists of Vitamins A, C, E, and K, and B6 for eye, pores and pores and skin, and mind fitness. Moreover, folate is one of the vitamins in spinach that allows your cardiovascular tool, and the magnesium in it maintains your blood strain at a wholesome diploma. If you're capable of educate your youngsters to consume veggies like spinach regularly, you can now not simplest hold coins from growing your non-public meals but in medicinal pills as properly.

Spinach can be planted in your raised mattress and the minimal requirement is 8 to 10 inches deep. You can plant them in a row 30 centimeters other than each special. When the usage of seedlings, deal with the roots cautiously due to the reality they're very satisfactory and fibrous as a manner to tear very without difficulty.

Watering must be your primary precedence with this plant; their leaves want to be saved moisturized, and so do the soil. Fish emulsions or compost tea are recommended to apply in location of fertilizers for better yield.

Also, you want to have a look at out for pests and worms. As spinach is a leafy vegetable, it can trap loads of worms and bugs, and they may use the leaves as nests for his or her larvae. Pick off the leaves whose undersides have white streaks of larvae. You can use garlic cleaning cleaning soap spray to do away with them or spinosad, an natural antibacterial implement, to save you in addition pests from attacking.

You can harvest your spinach leaves in lots less than a month, clean! You can use this same planting technique for lettuce as nicely.

Carrots

Carrots are an top notch deliver of Vitamin A, Vitamin C, calcium, fiber, carotene, zinc, manganese, fiber, and folate. When you consume at least 1/2 a cup of carrots every day, you'll no longer want those nutrients pills. Alternatively, you may make a carrot shake or smoothie to make swallowing a whole lot much less difficult.

Carrots can are also available first-rate solar shades like yellow, purple, and pink. The crimson range has a very precise antioxidant, which is also the motive of its one of a type color. You can ask for seeds or seedlings of those specific carrot species from the farmer's marketplace.

Raised beds and deep pots are quality for growing carrots and awesome root crops. Anything with a depth of extra than 12 inches is sufficient for carrots. You can plant several seeds, as a whole lot as four sources, in every one-inch rectangular; it is masses for one pot or raised bed.

However, carrot seeds are tiny, and you could lose control of what number of you put in one location. So, in reality let them enlarge before thinning or decreasing out the smaller leaves to expand more potent ones. Like one in all a type cold-climate plants, the soil desires to be moisturized frequently. Never allow the floor dry. They additionally determine upon free or loamier soil.

Within 14 days, the carrots will sprout however the reality that carrots are sensitive to common changes in weather conditions. To counter these results, area them wherein they might get sufficient breeze and daylight hours. The tremendous temperature is 13 levels Celsius. And voila, in handiest 2 to two and a half of months, you'll have your homegrown carrots to your plates! Harvest them with the aid of grasping the leafy tops and gently wiggling them out of the soil. The more youthful the carrots, the sweeter they will be.

The equal planting techniques is probably carried out to distinctive root crops including beets, potatoes, and radishes.

Onions

As each person recognise, onions are like tomatoes. They are essential for making your food flavor super. The pinnacle element with onions is that you could use each the bulb and the leaves. This is a completely low protection and actually speedy-developing plant. You can plant multiple seeds in a unmarried pot or bottle discipline, and you can simply snip the leaves and allow them to enlarge for terribly lengthy duration.

Onions can nearly increase in any box, however the most inexpensive manner is to plant them in plastic bottles. As for the soil, it's going to want a loamy soil enriched with compost. The faster manner to increase onions is to use transplants or glowing bulbs.

Place one bulb steady with three-inch square of the field. Bury them in reality into the soil until wherein the inexperienced coloration starts offevolved from the bulb. Onions require little care and renovation, excellent a cooler temperature and moist soil. If you need to fertilize, feed your onions with compost tea.

If you want to attain the bulbs, you will must wait until the tops begin to yellow and hunch. When this takes area, you have to bend the tops down similarly to save you the ripening. You'll ought to wait once more for the tops to expose brown earlier than you can pull the onion bulb, normally be cautious while doing this due to the reality the bulbs should likely bruise and rot. As the soil is wet, lay your bulbs to dry in advance than the use of them. You can also trim the leaves at the same time as the plant has reached 6 to 8 inches tall for the inexperienced onions.

Herbs

If there are herbs that thrive in a dry climate, these are the herbs that enlarge in bloodless weather situations:

- Parsley

- Coriander

- Dill

- Cilantro

Chapter 6: Gardening Tlc Lessons

Gardening isn't quite an awful lot plant life and boxes; many other elements make a plant grow, together with soil, weather, and the right gardening practices. Hence, here are a few belongings you want to apprehend approximately looking after your plants.

Soil and Fertilizer Ingredients

Your flora won't expand without soil, however it also won't expand with without a doubt undeniable antique soil that we often see at the ground. It wishes to be a combination of nutrients, especially potassium, phosphorous, and nitrogen, conducive to planting.

Microorganisms are jogging together to release the crucial vitamins that'll keep your plant alive and developing. What is regularly utilized in gardening these days are soil mixes, a combination of herbal and minerals that aids water go with the flow, airflow, decontamination, and vitamins. Some of the factors in a everyday soil mix are:

Organic depend or decomposed rely

They provide the microorganisms for plant vitamins and fitness.

Limestone

This regulates the pH ranges of the soil and includes calcium and magnesium to the plant life.

Sand

Aids water flow.

Peat moss

Retains water to keep soil moisturized in addition to enhancing drainage.

Vermiculite

Mineral flakes that amplify to help in aerating and water flowing in the ground.

Fertilizers are people who include nitrogen, phosphorus, and potassium (N-P-K). Each plant has top notch nutritional dreams, so while you purchase your fertilizer, understand what your plant needs, and look at the compost label.

The label need to offer you with three numbers, which advise the amount of N-P-K there may be for every mixture. Even despite the fact that herbal fertilizers are costly, they may be although maximum famous. This is specifically due to the fact they have NPK and one of a kind micronutrients much less in all likelihood to damage the soil and the plant roots.

Natural Insecticides and Pesticides

When you begin your garden, anticipate to supply other species worried aside from plant life. This is a natural incidence and now not some issue you want to be scared of, but it should be controlled; otherwise, high-quality those pests will advantage out of your vegetation.

The "3 sisters garden" approach includes arranging person flora in a single box due to the reality they help every high-quality expand. Similarly, you may use one plant's protection mechanism to defend the alternative flora. They have a natural capability to discourage wonderful sorts of pests, so what you can do is surround that plant at the side of the plant which attracts the pests.

You also can use biological controls or dwelling organisms to fight in the direction of the dwelling organisms attacking your plants. Some of those organic controls are spinosad, nematodes, milky spores, and Bt. You also can use herbal oils in choice to spraying chemical pesticides; these consist of: neem oil, garlic oil, pyrethrin, and summer season oils, which is probably plant and human-tremendous. All of these are to be had in maximum gardening stores.

Chapter 7: Hydroponics and Urban Renewal

What is hydroponics?

Hydroponics is a very exciting term. It's been around for quite some time now, however basically in a nutshell, it's the approach of growing flowers in a circulate of vitamins, but with out soil. The nutrient stuffed water flows via the trays. The flowers take inside the water, and the greater water flows to a barrel under.

That's basically what it's miles, growing vegetation in a movement of nutrients, this is the alternative of what traditional agriculture does.

How is hydroponics unique from metropolis agriculture?

It's very crucial to realize the distinction. Most "metropolis renewal" efforts interest on metropolis agriculture. This is likewise referred to as "town gardens" or network gardens. Both of these are fantastic, but the trouble lies in the reality that they're seasonal, and they don't produce sustainable jobs.

Hydroponics, however, is producing meals 24 hours a day, twelve months a one year. In Toledo, Ohio, in which I am from, we've what you call cold winters. For many folks that are supportive of city agriculture and community gardens, that's in which they forestall

With hydroponics, healthy meals can surely be grown 24 hours an afternoon, and that is what we're doing 365 days a year in Toledo, Ohio.

How a good buy does a growing unit rate?

This varies from group to organization. We artwork with a nice institution, Crop King, who materials our gadgets and we will communicate approximately that later. We're talking approximately near a $100,000 funding, but that doesn't embody the LED lighting, which makes this method so charming. You're talking approximately a $a hundred,000 unit; essentially, a $a hundred,000 investment for every growing unit.

Can you installation a growing unit interior and/or out of doors?

Yes. However, we're focusing on indoor gardens. That's one of the values of jogging in the city community. That's our awareness: food, possibility, and desire. We started out out setting food developing gadgets at a domestically owned greenhouse that has been in existence for over 30 years. We have thinking about the fact that improved operations to the Erie Street Market in downtown Toledo, Ohio.

Our motive is to develop indoor gardens. In most urban agencies throughout the u . S . A ., there are loads of vacant houses. Growing gadgets may be set up on vacant masses, however, within the Midwest and pretty some different locations, those growing devices can't virtually be blanketed.

Another hassle with vacant hundreds is the lack of protection. If there isn't a few aspect in vicinity to guard those gardens, alas, they will be destroyed. Aside from the ones issues, but, it may be carried out.

In segment 2, of this metropolis approach, the plan is to place devices inner empty homes and on vacant masses. I want to do this not most effective proper right here in Toledo, but throughout the u . S . A ..

Where do you buy the devices?

We artwork with a collection known as Crop King. There are special great groups accessible. Crop King sees and is aware of what we're seeking to do in phrases of sustainability and scalability. We'll talk about that later within the e-book.

Crop King knows our wishes. We're running with them and we need to maintain to artwork with them. They have notable products. They get the meals devices to you internal a consider form of days. You don't need to attend months and months, this is why we've decided on to artwork with Crop King

What is LED lighting?

LED lights is an exciting term. A plant can basically photosynthesize itself with LED lights. The (LED) lights produce crimson, blue, and white rays of slight, all of which is probably inside the spectrum of moderate the flora want to broaden fantastic.

Is LED lighting fixtures strength efficient?

As stated earlier than, we began out out with the useful resource of partnering with an present greenhouse. It's outstanding to start off that way, but, the fee to preserve emerge as past our price range. We will speak about that later. One of the problems with walking internal a greenhouse is the truth that it bleeds loads of electricity.

However, the cool element about LED lights is that it is very energy green. Because of the efficiency, we're capable of take advantage of hydroponics inside the wintry weather, in which maximum special efforts, like city agriculture, are near down.

Does hydroponics lessen water consumption?

Actually, it does. That's every other first-rate problem approximately beginning a "green business employer". It reduces the water consumption thru at the least an eighth. That's what I'm in fact captivated with.

We have seen that there's now not an entire lot of water intake in phrases of hydroponics. By the use of hydroponics, we use lots less water and preserve a everyday quantity of vitamins flowing to the plant life. Again, hydroponics makes use of an 8th of the water that could be utilized by a ordinary soil-primarily based really garden.

What veggies have to I grow first?

We've accomplished research on this, and lettuce is the number one produced vegetable right now. So, we're growing lettuce as we communicate. We've been doing this for about 8 months. It's time tested, meaning we have examined and established this for the past 8 months. The garden that we're growing indoors proper at the Erie Street Market, produces three,000+ heads of lettuce every week, pretty a few which go to neighborhood meals shops. Our reason, however, is to deliver 9,000-15,000 every week.

Our most vital form of lettuce is a natural hybrid product called Buttercrunch lettuce; it's scrumptious. It emerge as superior purposely for indoor boom, but it's now not genetically modified, and that's vital. Genetically changed lettuce does not exist.

In addition to the Buttercrunch lettuce, we expand Basil and Romaine lettuce. We'll be which incorporates tomatoes in a few months. Also, we're developing Mustard Greens, Collard Greens, and one-of-a-type produce that many human beings, within the city network, love. I'm truly pumped about that as properly.

To whom do you promote your produce?

We have a big again give up, 0.33 celebration, clients who're searching out our meals. Not best proper here in Ohio, but in Michigan as nicely.

There are lots of humans interested by buying our produce, which incorporates fitness food stores and close by farmers. Our ingredients also are used in hundreds of network restaurants. Recently, we moved into the farmer's market in downtown Toledo, Ohio.

How an lousy lot meals can those indoor gardens produce?

Right now we are generating 3,000 heads of lettuce in step with week. For each ½ acre garden, three whole-time and 3 element-time employees are required.

That's why it's far crucial that we function ourselves for instant growth. Our cutting-edge-day goal is to increase our developing region with the beneficial resource of a ½ acre every month. In our present day vicinity, we are generating nine,000 heads of lettuce in keeping with week.

In the close to similarly, we're able to be up to fifteen,000 heads of lettuce each week!

How do you decide the amount of nutrients the plants reap?

That takes a technological information. We have remarkable growers who inform me that each one of the trays have dripping nutrients. It's a very mild flow of vitamins going via the developing device, which flows slightly downhill to a drain inside the lower lower back, all the way down the 2 hundred-foot lawn.

Basically, the nutrients are split up into barrels. The manipulate device permits the grower to decide how lots nutrient-wealthy water the flora receive. It's sort of a technology. You have to watch it.

Each one of the trays has a completely light waft of vitamins streaming via the tool. Our men, because of the reality they've had such experience, decide the quantity on an afternoon-via the usage of the use of-day basis.

How prolonged does it take to set up a growing unit?

I assume that end up one in every of our stressful situations. We concept we should do it in more than one days, however our first developing unit took multiple weeks to hold together. Our men are sporting many hats. They're now not just growers. Danny and Brian are capable of accumulate subjects together as nicely.

Our 2d growing unit, but, most effective took a few hours. It didn't take extended once they determined a manner to do it.

How does hydroponics help in town renewal?

Most town organizations, in the course of the usa and international, are certainly asking questions: how can we offer sustainable close by jobs, and the way will we provide sustainable monetary opportunities?

One factor I count on many human beings have disregarded, city planners and those who are worried approximately town renewal, is that hydroponics is not simply supplying wholesome meals that we want, specifically in our city communities in which obesity and diabetes are rampant.

It is likewise a tool which can provide financial possibility. This entire new company of city farmers honestly offers an possibility for humans to have, not terrific correct wholesome meals, however sustainable jobs. It will become the financial model that we take delivery of as actual with can be proven in plenty of town regions spherical america of a

Here in Toledo we're already thinking about that. We accept as true with this model is every sustainable and scalable.

How many roles can the hydroponics commercial business enterprise produce?

Each 1/2-acre lawn requires three entire-time and three issue-time human beings. Our purpose is to increase growing place through 1/2 of an acre in line with month. We would love to have at the least two hundred people in the next 3 to five years.

Currently, we've got young folks who are working with us for the summertime proper here in Toledo, Ohio. We've hired approximately 5 personnel for now. We have more than one growers. These are young people which can be inquisitive about metropolis agriculture.

For many, it will become an opportunity career path on the same time as kids graduate from immoderate university. Right now, we're paying them $11.00 an hour, that is over and above the minimum profits.

That is one purpose why I need to get this e-book out: we are without a doubt trying out this model and it is working. What a awesome way to offer jobs, now not satisfactory for the summer, but all 12 months lengthy.

How is hydroponics specific from conventional farming?

The distinction is we growth meals above soil. Most conventional farmers must spend masses of time weeding. We don't have to do that. They want to position the seed inside the floor. I'm no longer knocking our farmers, however even as you reflect onconsideration on this whole "inexperienced motion," we want to do not forget the fitness of our planet. So, this may come to be a splendid "inexperienced industrial company" for social entrepreneurs.

In many times, the ground is clearly being raped with insecticides and such things as that. With hydroponics, we're developing above soil and defensive mom earth. It is nutrient primarily based, and it's located into little trays. I think that's the primary distinction: conventional depends at the soil, and we don't.

Is this generation being utilized in extraordinary international places?

Actually, it's far. A lot of it's miles being applied in precise parts of the vicinity. The Netherlands have used it. Jim Bloom, who I associate with at Sustainable Local Foods, discusses this in element at www.SustainableLocalFoods.Com. You also can touch me at William.James@SustainableLocalFoods.Com.

The Netherlands have followed this model, and it's moreover been finished in Europe. One of the primary issues Mr. Bloom stated he confronted whilst we first began this end up adapting to the strength systems used in the Netherlands. He spent some of time studying this method over the last 4 years.

We had been able to adopt this version with the aid of the usage of LED lights so the flowers can photosynthesize within the constructing. They've been the use of it all of the global over for quite some time. We desired to make sure that we take gain of this proper here inside the Midwest.

Also, a number of this hydroponics manner is being utilized in a number of the rural regions in our u . S .. It's essentially automated. There's not a physical presence there. We've taken that concept and translated it to the urban network, in which we can in fact get our our bodies involved who can be part of the gadget, with the intention of financial renewal and interest introduction.

Are the flora produced pesticide-free?

Yes. That's truly what I love approximately what we're doing in phrases of indoor gardening. Even inside, flora can expand natural issues and illnesses, however with Sustainable Local Foods, we develop organically, and we don't use any chemical pesticides on our plant life.

We use natural insecticides, along side ladybugs. This is referred to as "IPM," Integrated Pest Management. As our growers say, we rely on critters that devour exclusive critters. For each hassle, there's a solution that's herbal and doesn't require spraying chemical materials.

What are the one-of-a-type substances which are grown?

Right now we're developing Romaine and Buttercrunch lettuce, because that's the number one vegetable that maximum humans are looking for. We also are developing Basil and Collard Greens. We will broaden Tomatoes and Berries subsequent ye

Where is the satisfactory region to begin a developing unit?

I expect the exquisite area to start out, if you could, is with an present greenhouse. It's running for us. The disadvantage is that it bleeds pretty some electricity. Later on, we'll speak approximately "strength inexperienced greenhouses," this is some issue that we're jogging closer to developing.

In phrases of distribution, we at SLF would really like to partner with a number of you entrepreneurs to help get the phrase out approximately food possibilities and hope, at the equal time as developing a "boat load" of money at the same time!

Chapter 8: The Challenges of the Urban Community

What are some of the dangers of city neighborhoods?

Of course we recognize commonly its crime. We have gang violence. Many marketers and organizations have moved out of the city community because of those sorts of things. There's no longer masses of choice, and that's what we're searching for to offer: opportunities and want.

Buildings are falling aside and there are numerous empty masses. We see this as an opportunity for transformation. We can also even speak about dangerous food practices which have produced weight problems and diabetes, that is a big hassle in lots of urban corporations.

When you're now not feeling pinnacle and also you're no longer looking right, that might add to the troubles and demanding conditions of an city network.

What are a number of the advantages of metropolis neighborhoods?

In most town agencies we are able to repurpose houses and insert growing gadgets.

During that technique of repurposing we will rent humans to assist repurpose some of the ones homes. In most urban businesses, there's already a bit force in area. Many humans are taught get right of entry to-degree positions, the way to do simple paintings, and we are capable of take that and apply it to the city farming business enterprise.

There are severa benefits to having growing gadgets within the city community, in particular right proper here in Toledo, Ohio. In truth, we've got got were given devices in our downtown place at the Erie Street Market. This became a place at the beginning intended for dispensing meals. It have been abandoned for a while. Now, we're searching for to supply the Market decrease lower back to its actual cause, with hydroponics. We see that there are greater advantages as opposed to dangers in the city regions.

What are the outcomes of volatile food on urban citizens?

Unhealthy food produce risky attitudes. If you don't experience right about yourself, you're lethargic, you're worn-out, and also you don't have plenty strength. If you're no longer consuming nicely, you're no longer looking well.

Unfortunately, in many town areas there are not supermarkets. Instead, there are convenience shops that sell Twinkies and unique sugary treats. There aren't any grocery shops which have reasonably-priced healthy meals. Not handiest can we no longer have much less highly-priced wholesome food, but we're no longer taught in the town network a manner to prepare the ones types of meals.

To make subjects worse, maximum of those consolation shops aren't in reality stocked with wholesome components. This is unfortunate. It does produce a terrible impact on our attitudes, on our disposition, and on our outlook. When I say on us, I'm talking about the ones people inside the metropolis network.

I pastor inside the town community and I even have become raised in the town community. We have for-income and non-earnings which might be designed to help urban citizens. The hassle of weight issues keeps re-going through time and again all over again. In fact, I grow to be looking at an article no longer too lengthy within the past in Science Daily.

It basically stated that lower-income neighborhoods are associated with better weight problems rates. This changed into some years in the past once more in 2008. They positioned that neighborhoods with decreased financial and social sources have higher prices of weight problems.

They furthermore determined that residents in low-income town regions are much more likely to document more network boundaries to bodily activity, at the side of confined opportunities for each day walking and reduced get right of get admission to to to shops that promote wholesome ingredients, particularly large supermarkets.

That's clearly awesome to me. Not lengthy ago a fellow from Chicago through the call of Ken Dunn, who runs a recycling and concrete gardening company, came to Toledo. He stated that we've have been given many property due to the reality we have were given an entire lot of available vacant land and manpower. I might take a look at with that manpower because the already made artwork pressure that you and I referred to.

These vacant houses can assist in constructing a sturdy nearby meals machine so that it will help heal those low-earnings corporations.

That's why I'm obsessed with what we're doing in terms of growing sustainable healthful meals in metropolis groups. Gallup did a survey not long ago and they predicted that 80 billion dollars in line with 3 hundred and sixty 5 days are spent on health prices due to fitness troubles collectively with weight problems and diabetes.

Treating diabetes and weight issues in the city network can charge an entire lot of cash.

What are the benefits of eating healthful food?

You experience higher. You have a higher outlook. You're extra proactive, and also you're energized. I try to devour sensibly. I be aware that after I'm consuming ordinary cease result and veggies I actually have a greater great proactive mind-set, I want to get subjects finished.

I truely have greater electricity. If you're not eating well meals and you're continuously consuming Twinkies and cupcakes, you're lethargic and don't have lots of a electricity. That now not exceptional affects us in my opinion, but it additionally affects a community if the human beings are not consuming wholesome meals.

We need to show more of our metropolis groups to healthy food on a ordinary sustainable foundation. I love metropolis agriculture, and I love community gardens. I love the efforts that we're seeing at some stage in america of america and even across the world in plenty of our town regions.

But, they're in reality not sustainable. They may work throughout the summer season months, and that's excellent. It exposes many to wholesome ingredients, however we want a few element more sustainable.

We want to take it to scale. We need as a way to provide healthy materials constantly. I suppose hydroponics takes it to the subsequent degree.

Imagine a 24-hour meals manufacturing website online, one year a one year at a few level in the u . S . In our metropolis environments!

We are taking healthful consuming and healthy living to each other degree. I'm enthusiastic about the efforts that we're making in Toledo, Ohio.

Most town neighborhoods attention on urban agriculture, additionally known as metropolis Ag, or network gardens as an answer for economic empowerment.

This is because of the fact they have got no longer been uncovered to hydroponics. Hydroponics may be highly-priced. That's why I love the imaginative and prescient of Sustainable Local Foods. You can research extra approximately what we're doing at www.SustainableLocalFoods.Com. Also, you can contact me at William.James@SustainableLocalFoods.Com.

There are some films and pictures at the internet site approximately what we're doing. When coronary coronary heart-focused business employer human beings like Jim Bloom and Nick, his son, who's the CEO, have a imaginative and prescient for healthy food and sustainable jobs, then we are capable of get those gadgets shifting forward.

I admire non-income. I actually have a non-earnings and we're on foot with Sustainable Local Foods. But, I think so as for "monetary renewal" to take vicinity, pretty some our for-income must take the lead. Fortunately, Sustainable Local Foods has the investment to assist this anointed task.

The hassle internal most of our urban groups is, we're recycling and redistributing wealth, but now not growing it. We'll communicate greater about that when we get into the whole financial aspect of metropolis gardening.

Why are most metropolis neighborhoods focused on brief-time period fixes as opposed to lengthy-time period fixes in phrases of monetary renewal?

I want to get into extra of that once we talk about financial technique. I assume the quick strategy to this is, we're now not questioning long-term. We're wondering quick fixes. We're thinking about placing bandages on issues, but we are not virtually fixing the troubles.

We have instant needs to get jobs in our community. Many of our corporations are genuinely targeted in the community. We're now not considering taking our groups outdoor of wherein we are.

There is likewise the problem of sustainability. Sustainability could be very crucial to me close to an prolonged-term monetary model. Sustainability is defined as some thing that may maintain. It's now not quick-term. If we are able to do it right proper right here, we will take it on the road.

Unfortunately, many speedy meals eating places and precise corporations internal our metropolis corporations are not centered on long time. I recognize right right right here in Toledo we have extra eating places consistent with capita than in all of the United States. They'll run out of enterprise enterprise after or 3 years and the following eating place will update them.

There's not a centered try to make it sustainable and scalable: Scalable which means that as a manner to take the "show on the street" and placed it in distinct corporations. We'll get greater into that once we talk approximately growing an financial method.

Currently, in most town regions there is not a long term monetary approach for renewal. We're looking for to control immediately dreams, with out searching in the path of economic empowerment. I expect that is the actual trouble.

How can we inspire entrepreneurship in metropolis organizations?

You need to create an surroundings for ownership. I count on that is definitely the mission. We're no longer honestly encouraging entrepreneurship. This first rate u . S . Of ours changed into based on small groups. We have to create an environment for entrepreneurship. We'll speak about that once we speak community of partners.

It is essential to recognize that renewal starts with the authorities and one in every of a type "anchor groups." Their involvement will create the surroundings so that it will make it lots less complex for small corporations to flourish.

There are hundreds of special jobs in town agriculture, like transportation, control, and so forth.

This is probably one degree of the city renewal technique in phrases of a valid monetary technique. It's crucial at SLF to have humans begin their non-public companies.

We'll communicate extra about this later. We can encourage entrepreneurship in the areas of people proudly owning their very personal meals-developing devices and making $40,000-60,000 a 12 months. That's kind of section 2 of what we're seeking to do.

I would really like to ask those studying this e-book to the touch me, due to the truth we're attempting out the possession part of our approach. That's section 2. That's how you're making it sustainable, thru using raising up companies.

To me, part of the definition of an extended-time period financial approach method it's to be had for all, even folks which are popping out of jail or maybe our veterans.

That's what I love about this undertaking. It consists of all of us. We've created a plan to do that, and I'm obsessed on renewing and rekindling this spirit of entrepreneurship in city regions. This is essential to us at Sustainable Local Foods.

Why are we not focusing at the issues of sustainability and scalability in urban neighborhoods?

It's the short-time period repair. We're on the lookout for to positioned fires out. For many humans it's hard to keep in mind thriving while they'll be simply in search of to live on. I assume many businesses, unluckily, have not centered on the prolonged-time period.

We must think about approaches to not handiest start a enterprise, however to make it sustainable and scalable. In order to do this, you want to expect through an monetary version that does really that.

That's what I love about healthful ingredients. It's not pretty much wholesome food. It's moreover turning into a model. Hydroponics is growing and producing prolonged-time period healthful ingredients. It turns into a model for financial renewal that produces the outcome of sustainability and scalability.

I've in no manner visible a version that has this type of functionality, and I'm excited about it!

How is the wholesome food version every sustainable and scalable?

When we remember meals, that's virtually the not unusual denominator. People are commonly going to devour food. We've been ingesting food whilst you take into account that the start of time. It's just a splendid nice of food. People are generally going to have a need to eat.

The problem then will become how do we take this meals and tie it into an financial plan? That's what we're doing proper here in Toledo with Sustainable Local Foods.

Urban farming now creates opportunities, similarly to an opportunity career route for people to pursue. In the Midwest we're tormented by this whole vehicle crunch in which the automobile enterprise is up and down. I be given as true with that city farming can come along our businesses and help to create employment opportunities.

Right now we have a outstanding possibility to build a robust, wholesome infrastructure in healthful meals and prolonged-term jobs. After 8 months now, we're as it's viable.

This is what I name building the food agency and offering monetary opportunities. When we're talking approximately sustainability and scalability, what you're definitely speakme approximately is preference for our town community.

That is our reason: not to genuinely produce network healthy elements, but to offer possibilities and need. That is what we're doing in Toledo.

Why are most urban agencies no longer scalable?

Because maximum enterprise proprietors are not asking the query of techniques they're capable of take a services or products out of doors their specific place of effect.

Franchises try and try this, however irrespective of a number of the franchises we see in Toledo, they're focused on certain geographical areas of the metropolis. There now not thinking Detroit, MI, this is proper down the street. It's only a neighborhood reputation.

With this "social version" that exists in most town regions, wealth is being redistributed instead of created. Our reason is to elevate marketers with a thoughts-set of sustainability and scalability.

For many organisation proprietors the bottom line is earnings. However, we decide upon the "Triple Bottom Line" as our model. That's what social marketers do.

I see myself as a "pastorpreneur", a pastor who wants to construct the nearby church but additionally collect the network at the same time. Social marketers take a look at troubles and are seeking out to resolve them on a large scale via making them more effective.

Again, we're no longer just specializing inside the backside line, that is income for maximum groups. We're moreover focusing at the people and the planet. I think if you have that Triple Bottom Line coming to the table, it most effective forces you to bear in mind a long time marketing and marketing approach.

How would possibly you define inner cities?

Inner cities are distressed metropolis corporations. The terms are interchangeable. Any time there may be monetary despair or any time that you have short-time period jobs or can't find out a manner, that's the inner metropolis.

Who is my neighbor?

That's a superb query, and I must spend all day discussing this critical trouble. I did a Ph. D dissertation at the complete concept of the neighbor in Aberdeen, Scotland.

My neighbor is anybody who's in want of humanity. I'm not without a doubt positive to the neighbor who is close to, folks that percentage a similar experience, or percentage my equal ethnicity.

I'm advantageous not most effective to the neighbor who's close to but also to the neighbor who is a protracted way, individuals who are out of doors my life-style, similarly to individuals who are out of doors my revel in.

The neighbor will become the moral criterion for me. To deny my neighbor is to deny myself. I anticipate it's critical to understand who my neighbor is, in particular due to the truth, God has placed my neighbor there to task me and to job my memory that I don't exist on my own.

I exist in what I name "co-humanity." It's an ontological reality, in which following policies is a commandment to have a look at. As I am sure to you, you're positive to me. To deny you is to deny me.

To the various coronary coronary heart-centered agency individuals who are analyzing this e-book, and may be reluctant to do business enterprise within the city community, we have been demonstrating how the advantages overwhelm the horrific additives.

You can make an entire lot of cash on the town hydroponics. We'll get into that when we get into the whole monetary piece, growing your economic method. I'm excited to talk approximately that. But it starts offevolved offevolved with that fundamental query, who is my neighbor?

My neighbor is absolutely everyone who's in want. My neighbor is every person who wants to have their dignity upheld. That's not simplest a biblical time period. Jesus requested this query, who is my neighbor? The neighbor is a traditional ethical criterion.

To deny you is to deny me. We have been made to exist, "co-humanity."

Why is figuring out the answer to this query of "Who is my neighbor?" essential for town renewal?

Again, if I don't apprehend that the neighbor is the moral criterion for me, that the neighbor determines whether or not or no longer or now not I'm being moral or no longer, that the neighbor in truth gadgets the criterion and isn't just some part of a fixed of policies that announces I must be quality to people, then many businesses will stay away from metropolis areas.

I'm speakme approximately right coronary coronary heart-centered enterprise folks who want to make a distinction. They will not allow the things that they've heard approximately the city community, the crime and violence, deter them far from doing industrial enterprise.

When I apprehend that my neighbor is not most effective the neighbor who is close, but also the neighbor who's a ways, who may additionally moreover live at the alternative issue of the train tracks, I am but positive to them.

If I don't maintain that in mind, it will not simplest preserve me from serving individuals who stand out of doors of my subculture or out of doors of my financial reputation, but it could keep me from understanding that there's a extremely good opportunity to do commercial employer and to installation more relationships.

Many parents simplest have some buddies. However, as we are in search of for to do metropolis renewal, as we searching for to conform without this plan that we're providing with introducing healthful food, presenting jobs, and raising up urban farmers, you may find out that, as a commercial employer person, you can expand relationships on a whole new level.

I anticipate human beings want to have wholesome relationships. Those relationships are not just set up in my non-public sphere of have an impact on. I keep in mind that God wants to introduce us to a purchasers of friends that we'd in no way commonly see on our each day walk.

What does it suggest to like my neighbor as myself?

If I fee myself, I'm going to price others. It's difficult to like others and fee others if I don't love myself. I'm not speakme approximately a self-targeted love, that's egocentric.

I'm speaking about an appreciation of the truth that God has made each you and me precise in our personal manner. We all have strengths and weaknesses. But, we were made inside the picture of God.

If you could appreciate who you are, you'll be able to respect who others are. A lot of that is the way you notice yourself, how you're raised, and particularly how one eats.

Remember that the trouble of this e-book is Urban Gardening. I be given as proper with, if you consume better food, you've got had been given more readability in the way you agree with you studied. A lot of our thinking and perceptions are clouded because of the truth we are ingesting food which may be awful for us.

That's one of the matters that we're praying for within the course of this approach, that God could genuinely do a miracle with our taste buds. I realize I'm doing that in my family. I pray to God to without a doubt redirect our flavor buds to in which we've got got a taste for whole, wholesome food, in vicinity of unhealthy elements.

Many oldsters are so whole of pollution, and now not just bodily pollution. I be given as actual with there may be a dating some of the pollutants in our our our bodies and poisonous relationships. I think that wholesome self-love lets you recognize others as nicely.

I've travelled all over the global. One element I've found out is that God loves variety. I earned my Ph. D in Aberdeen, Scotland, and I enjoyed appealing with humans outdoor of my lifestyle.

I've discovered out that, at the surrender of the day, humans want to be preferred. People want to be affirmed, and we in reality are a "one-international" community. God loves range.

One way to bridge "the relational hole" is the everyday commonplace denominator of meals, and that's what we're looking to do at some stage in this approach. I'm excited.

Why do you positioned there aren't any supermarkets in most city neighborhoods?

I've usually been concerned approximately this growing up, considering we in desired have nook or convenience stores. I suppose from a commercial enterprise attitude, many those who open these supermarkets don't enjoy that people within the city communities can pay for his or her products.

Please apprehend, for the purpose of this speak, with regards to healthful meals, many metropolis citizens can't have enough money it. Many consolation stores are installation and people are shopping for reasonably-priced candy bars and Twinkies for seventy five cents or a greenback.

I'm amazed at how lots coins human beings make with those comfort stores, due to the reality they're reasonably-priced. You can pass in and get a incredible amount of junk meals for pennies on the dollar. In the summertime, you could get a slushy or a soda pop.

During the summer time in Toledo, Ohio, you could get a big pop for subsequent to nothing. When it entails health food, it's the problem of affordability.

Again, they're on hand and, as an proprietor, you could make a quick greenback. Whereas with supermarkets, you're going to need to spend a bit bit more. Unfortunately, cash isn't being produced. It's absolutely being recycled from paycheck to paycheck.

We'll speak approximately this entire "economic version" rather than the "social version" at the same time as we get into the talk of developing an economic technique. We're not raising marketers which might be capable of generate wealth interior city businesses. Let's not overlook about that the hope issue of this city renewal technique is to raise the ones marketers who can create wealth in the city context.

These are brief-recuperation answers and that they're now not centered on the overall fitness of the town areas. These solutions are for the ones folks that need to make quick money.

Would you are saying this is why Toledo metropolis citizens have struggled with weight troubles, especially amongst our young adults?

Absolutely!

They're literally right there in the front parents, those comfort stores. If you strain in most city corporations, you'll see them. They're right there, those consolation shops.

I think in phrases of weight problems, Toledo, Ohio have become ranked amount seven out of all the maximum obese towns inside the United States.

Thirty- percentage of Toledo citizens are managing weight problems problems. Again, in comparison to the cities in the United States, we are ranked big range seven, and I think an lousy lot of this is due to those comfort shops which can be determined on every nook.

People are just putting out, consuming pop, and eating rapid meals. It creates a few awesome community, but it produces horrible consuming behavior, and we see the awful consequences of that.

Anytime you don't experience right approximately your self and also you're not looking your awesome, it adds to the general dangers of loads of our town companies in phrases of productiveness.

What have you and your organisation carried out to assist assignment weight issues, particularly amongst young human beings in Toledo, Ohio?

We have these days partnered with (TPS), Toledo Public Schools, which feeds approximately 20,000 children a day. It's first-rate.

Starting in 2015, we have topics in region in which we'll be able to offer healthy materials for his or her menus. We additionally offer food to folks who are hungry in our surrounding agencies.

We best place those growing gadgets in town businesses in which human beings don't have transportation. We accept as real with in tithing. Tithe manner 10 percent. We tithe 10 percentage of our standard produce lower again into the network.

We're tough our students and supporting them to consume higher in 2015. We're giving meals away. We're providing an possibility career route. We have younger human beings at SLF who're exploring city farming. They're capable of see this complete system from planting a seed to acquire.

We're elevating the charge of healthful ingredients with the useful resource of the usage of bringing them to urban companies on an extended-time period basis. We are doing the entirety from giving food away to partnering with public faculty systems. We'll show you a manner to try this if you need greater statistics.

We are offering possibilities for human beings to be around this complete metropolis agricultural meals gadget, in addition to, raising the fee of wholesome ingredients..

How does offering a career path in town farming teach extra younger people the importance of growing a organisation mind?

As I formerly said, we've got to expose them to it. With the economy proper now, I strive to tell younger humans that, you need to assume in terms of business possession.

No depend what profession you pick out out, you want to have a plan B. Be an entrepreneur or; very very very own your non-public industrial employer. Let's be actual, quite a few our more younger people are losing out of immoderate university or genuinely getting a excessive faculty diploma. They're no longer even going to college.

That doesn't advocate they're now not clever. That doesn't mean they don't have capacity. Within our agency, you do ought to research some topics, however you do not need to have a immoderate college diploma.

We're starting the door for veterans and ex-offenders. Obviously, we're now not trying to hire murderers. The difficulty is, however, city farming produces an possibility profession direction.

You can virtually begin to paintings your manner up the farming enterprise ladder. You can pass from transportation, to seeding, to packaging and in the long run you can in reality non-public your very very own growing unit.

You, as an person or as a own family, may also need to make $forty,000 a yr or even greater, and we can assist finance that. Why? Because we'll take the food this is grown and promote it to our again quit buyers.

You can virtually repay that unit in four or 5 years. Now you're placing coins apart and getting prepared for the future. We are rekindling the spirit of entrepreneurship, and that's what the town community desires.

What is the number one task that the city network have to triumph over?

Job advent. We have to produce jobs. This is the battle in many of our town environments: we do not have jobs. If we do have jobs, they're quick term, now not prolonged-time period.

We want to create jobs right away. We've been on this approach for nearly eight months now in Toledo, Ohio, and already we've created 5 to seven jobs. We're paying above minimum sales at $eleven an hour.

Why can we do this? It's due to the fact we've decrease returned prevent consumers. We have groups who need to shop for our produce. We make our meals much less costly. We must make a profits, we're a for-income, however it's far less highly-priced.

We have companies in Michigan standing in line pronouncing, "We'll take your food."

We want to develop Michigan as well, and distinct states, however we want every town to have its personal community presence. We're now not mixing apples and oranges. Food organizations are able to pay for our produce due to the fact we're generating food each couple of weeks. That's interesting!

That's what I love about hydroponics. It doesn't take lengthy to get the machine going, and you may start processing food proper!

Chapter 9: Creating a community of companions

Why do you need a network of companions for urban renewal?

Momentum actually. This isn't some component you want to do with the resource of your self. This is thrilling due to the fact that's the aim: To Create a Movement. That's the whole scale piece, a movement.

The greater you have got on board, this is our goal with this community of vision companions, the extra you can get finished. You cannot renew or revise a network through the usage of the usage of yourself.

You may also have amazing pursuits and a big coronary coronary heart, however you're going to get caught alongside the way. From the start, it modified into our reason to create a partnership through this method. We'll communicate approximately how some of the ones relationships may be very efficient. For the readers, you need to do this as nicely.

The greater humans which you have on board, the more you can produce. We're just beginning to see, even in this infancy level, that we have got this network of companions: people combating the equal purpose and those who're engaged on this movement. It allows us to leverage what we're looking for to do.

What form of companions do you want?

I expect you want Pastors, those within the spiritual sector. You want authorities human beings. You need to engage the urban network, due to the reality that's what it's all about. You need organisation human beings.

If you carry all of these groups collectively, you can see that healthful food is the missing link that brings all of those collectively.

I started placing some circles together on my wall in my place of work. I'm mapping this out in circles, in which I can see how these superb entities engage. Healthy meals surely becomes the missing hyperlink.

You can add partners along the manner, however the way we started is with five circles. If you may consider for your thoughts that those circles intersect in the middle, this type of circles want to be your community leaders: religious and the government. We'll communicate later about the way it's important to get community government on board.

You moreover have your coronary heart-targeted employer proprietors and your social entrepreneurs. Remember, they're each involved approximately humans and planet, and characteristic earnings as their bottom line.

Then one might likely need to welcome the inner city of path, that is what we're addressing, distressed town neighborhoods. If you placed those at the outdoor, definitely draw the ones circles together. Now, there's one circle inside the middle in which all of them intersect, and you'll see that healthful meals is in fact the "missing center". I like that time period, the "lacking middle", because of the truth that brings it all collectively.

We can amplify on the ones type of later, however what we've finished is we've reached out to those leaders. Even our mayor may be very supportive of what we're searching out to do right here. He sees this as something that has the functionality to be large in Northwest Ohio.

Mayor Collins have grow to be in recent times brought to our challenge and technology. He said, "SLP can provide preference and opportunity for our network."

We took him and his body of people on a tour, and he said that he's a organisation believer that that could be a current-day undertaking for this location inside the agricultural corporation. I love what the mayor said. He said, "He sees it as a capacity enterprise location of interest to complement all of the various matters which might be happening proper right here in Toledo."

The generation and technology pressure the growth of produce 3 hundred and sixty five days a year. When you discern our precise feature in the market, Mayor Collins said, "He ought to very without trouble see us gravitating in the direction of becoming a primary supplier to this corridor of the USA, from a commercial enterprise corporation area of interest factor of view."

It's clearly the start. It's some different footprint in northwest Ohio. It's a big possibility for business commercial enterprise organisation increase. Again, we want to take it an awful lot in addition than Northwest Ohio.

We need to installation the ones agencies of partners in considered one of a type areas for the duration of the u . S . As properly.

It's our aim to supply 200 jobs inside the Toledo region inside the subsequent five years. We're obsessed with that. Imagine what we can produce, alongside the way, in exclusive metropolis regions.

I want to reiterate that every half acre of developing region calls for 167 hours of labor each week. Think about that. This essentially manner that, Toledoans, and one-of-a-kind town corporations in particular, can purchase regionally and organically at the equal time as assisting Toledo personnel on this whole organisation of metropolis agriculture.

What are the roles that every partner performs?

The religious problem is vital for town renewal. I've been pastoring for 14 years in an city context. Our cause, and most pastors' cause, isn't always simply to have a spiritual impact, however we need to have an "existential impact," as well.

To oldsters which can be analyzing this book, you could not have a non secular history, but, I accept

114

as proper with you're analyzing through divine appointment. You are right proper right here to help me in this divine assignment!

Most non secular people, whether or not or now not you're a Christian or now not, if you're into spiritual enrichment, your purpose is to now not simply to make a non secular impact, however to make an existential impact as properly.

Our Bible says in Matthew 25 that if you deliver a cup of cold water in His name, Jesus says, "You have executed it unto me." You will see a reward for that. If you assist folks which are oppressed, you get credit score score score for that.

From a religious trouble, you want that non secular effect due to the truth which will encourage you to get a imaginative and prescient of the "united states" wherein to make an existential effect.

I these days sat down with Matt Sapara who's the Economic Director. I've positioned with most economic administrators, their revitalization plan will maximum in all likelihood encompass imparting interest and financial possibilities.

In my research, I clearly have seen the ones questions normally emerge as soon as I examine the town context: how are we able to provide long-term jobs? How can we provide prolonged-term financial opportunities?

Of route, the government is given a tremendous amount of cash to make that take location. You need your network leaders, after which of path your business corporation owners. If you could display them an possibility in which they cannot first-class assist people, but, also make money as nicely, they will buy in.

We'll speak approximately this more at the same time as we communicate the monetary techniques. Please recognize you can make a supply load of cash in phrases of hydroponics. Ninety 8 percentage of produce fed on with the resource of Toledoans comes from greater than 1,800 miles away. This way that simplest percentage of the produce that is being ate up is domestically grown.

Meanwhile, the City of Toledo has an unemployment rate of 5.7%. I want you to recognize that 98% produce that we eat, is being purchased from outside of Toledo. All we're saying with this "network of partners" is, to fight for network meals manufacturing!

In most Midwestern communities, we're best preserving 3 to 4 percent. Most of the fruits and greens that we're consuming on an annual basis are coming from outdoor our town, outdoor our kingdom.

You can also even want the internal metropolis to continuously remind us and maintain us at the pulse of what's taking place. They're constantly announcing, "We need extended-time period jobs, we need long-time period economic opportunities."

We want to look the treasure there, like repurposing and building on empty loads. There's charge there in case you glance through the eyes of the neighbor and notice the need.

Let me encourage you to volunteer to be a part of a close-by metropolis agriculture organization, folks which may be absolutely growing network gardens. You'll be capable of sense that people are hungry for alternate, actually hungry now not only for proper food, however for alternate.

You can see how those efforts encourage want. You deliver those circles together, community leaders authorities and spiritual, business enterprise proprietors, the internal town, and social marketers, folks which can be worried for extra than simply profit.

Social marketers are ChangeMakers. They need to do greater than absolutely make cash. They choice solutions for social ills, and that they do it on a big scale. Those are the shape of human beings on the table.

You carry them collectively and you may see the importance of ways get right of entry to to wholesome components will become the missing link. These are the sorts of relationships that deliver network companions together.

If you leverage the ones relationships, you could do some super things within the town areas.

How cannot having a collection of partners thwart your efforts?

You should depend on yourself. You need to depend on your very own electricity, your very personal plans. We all have blind spots, don't we? There are some matters we don't see.

When you interest in your dreams and your imaginative and prescient, it's a centered strive, but, there are some subjects that you omit. When we inventory a group together, we're able to play off of every particular's strengths.

Jim Bloom at Sustainable Local Foods and I actually have masses in not unusual. He introduced me to this entire idea. We want to honor God in a huge way, and we want to assist humans in a big manner.

He can see some subjects that I can't see and I can see a few matters he can't see. As the Bible says, "Iron Sharpens Iron." When you carry all of those entities to the desk, they complement each different.

To do subjects with the useful resource of your self, you will no longer get an entire lot momentum. There can be a few frustration inside the beginning. Jim and I, we laugh together and we get frustrated together, however we're shifting earlier. We are better together.

Again, you can't do it via yourself. We need to get past rugged individualism. Our purpose is to provide healthy city environments. This momentum is interesting: an individual network of companions operating together toward effective metropolis renewal.

We're all at the equal net net page. Many of us have tried to do renewal in precise techniques, but on the identical time as we concentrate our efforts, we see that get admission to to wholesome food is definitely the lacking hyperlink.

There's a contemporary electricity proper proper right here in Toledo. People are coming alive. Again, our intention isn't great to deliver wholesome components to the desk, however possibilities and preference as nicely.

Why is it critical to recognize your nearby community revitalization plan?

Because a number of you who're studying this records are commercial enterprise owners and a number of you are "social organization," you have got had been given both challenge and cash to be powerful. That's what I love approximately social commercial enterprise organisation.

There are human beings on hand with hundreds and hundreds and tens of thousands and lots of bucks, and I hope some of you are analyzing this book, due to the reality you could take a plan, and get subjects shifting because of the fact you have the greenbacks to decrease decrease again it up.

Remember, our intention is to take this across the place. When you deliver this all together, you should have a plan. I can also encourage everyone to sit down down down together with your financial director. Most cities have an monetary director.

Matt Sapara truly came into our place of work and he said, "That's the number one element on my schedule: to offer jobs and to offer monetary opportunities." That's the subject.

As I stated in advance, Mr. Sapara can see the monetary technique inside the again of our healthful meals model. It isn't simply imparting pinnacle components, however moreover supplying long time jobs.

He, along together with his teammates, stepped right on board. We've been rocking and rolling ever due to the reality that. Again, discover what your city community revitalization plan is, and let them understand what you're hoping to perform. We allow you to find out extra.

Visit our net net page at SustainableLocalFoods.Com; or go away a message with me at William.James@SustainableLocalFoods.Com. I would love to talk with you free of price. It's all about taking it spherical the arena.

Send your monetary director an e mail and permit him apprehend what you're looking to do.

Find out what his or her revitalization plan is, and then lay out what you're seeking to do. They'll bounce on board; I assure it.

Why does your group want to recognition on putting in place a "movement" for your community?

If it's not a movement, it will in reality be right right here nowadays and gone day after today. We don't want any "one-hit wonders". We're seeking to create a motion. We are frustrated with the useful resource of the reality that in most metropolis organizations, humans have a tough time looking after themselves and feeding their families.

It is appalling to me that during this extremely good u . S . There are people right here in Toledo who can't discover the cash for healthy food. At my church we're giving meals away. People are in reality going days without food, young and old. It's appalling.

If you don't make it a movement or a venture, then some factor is motivating you from an person mind-set, will in the long run lose its gas.

We're seeking to create a motion, now not best for this metropolis, however for the arena. This is the proactive mindset that we're taking. That's the mindset via which we're being lead.

To be honest, we want to shake up the metropolis community with what we're doing through hydroponics! We want to shake up the arena with this monetary method. We don't want all people suffering with get proper of get admission to to to meals, specifically healthy food.

We want human beings to have jobs. We need our younger human beings to have a future. We want to provide alternative career paths. We want to provide opportunities.

Again, we're looking this motion develop in Toledo in a few brief months. Because it's working proper right here, we are privy to it's going to art work everywhere. A motion keeps you inspired. A movement of companions who're saying, "We're putting pores and skin in the game, we're in it for the prolonged-term," come hell or immoderate waters, as we are announcing within the Christian international, we're going to stay the course.

A motion offers that shape of electricity, that shape of motivation, that form of pleasure to hold transferring in advance.

How is get admission to to healthy food the intersecting link?

As I said previously, it's lovely on many without a doubt considered one of a kind fronts. It's no longer in reality get proper of entry to to healthy substances, however ingredients which might be going to be to be had extended-term. Again, we don't have constant access to healthy elements in most metropolis groups.

We have efforts with metropolis gardening and community gardens, and we talked about that, but the ones are short-term, they're seasonal. It's no longer in reality lengthy-term.

Access to extended-time period healthful food allows us to no longer simplest provide substances which might be appropriate for us, that make us look higher and experience higher and do better, but it becomes the economic version to create sustainable, prolonged-term jobs.

Most humans do not recognise that hydroponics, producing our non-public materials 24 hours an afternoon, 3 hundred and sixty 5 days a year, can grow to be, and we're seeing it now, an financial method for revitalization in metropolis agencies.

Most humans have left out that. We've been capable of get a preserve of that. We take delivery of as actual with it's a God issue. Now we're going to now not first-rate do that in terms of what's taking place proper right here, but we're taking this display on the road.

How do I create those forms of relationships?

You need to make cellular phone calls. Again, we let you with that. Before we surely placed our first growing unit up a few months inside the past, we had been form of getting sidebars with humans and allowing them to understand.

In the start of this movement we didn't make a huge deal about what we had been doing. Here in Toledo, and in masses of different locations, human beings won't in reality guide you until they see matters happening. Even despite the fact that we mentioned what we desired to do, you may almost pay attention the "Yeah, yeah, yeah, we've heard that in advance than."

When we certainly went out and purchased a developing unit and began generating meals, we held off for some time. Over time, we invited the overall public to look. That's while the energy started out taking area. That's at the same time as the conversations and media started out to take place.

We're definitely doing it; we're now not definitely speaking about it. To the ones of you analyzing this e book, those conversations need to start proper away.

You want to begin considering a number of the relationships that you could have already got in region. Business owners, a number of you figure in government, and a number of you're pastorpreneurs.

I'm defining pastorpreneurs as the ones of you who are not really worried with constructing a healthful developing church, however you want to construct a wholesome growing community as properly.

You need to start having the ones discussions now, at the equal time as paying attention to the "heartbeat" of the inner city. Start task out to mother and father that you already recognize have a strength in your community and say, "This is something we're searching for to do. Will you purchase in? Will you're making a contribution? Will you be part of our community of companions?" You is probably amazed at their response.

People are looking for leadership. We're missing management. You don't need to be an expert to be the only that draws this entire hassle together. I don't recall myself an expert.

If you asked me approximately hydroponics a yr or so in the past, I ought to say, "What are you speaking about?" due to the fact I didn't recognize something about it. However, I usually characteristic myself to be geared up to make an existential effect in my community.

I accept as true with the celebs honestly coated up. God brought Jim Bloom and I collectively, and those are the shape of partnerships that may be duplicated everywhere in the united states of the usa, or everywhere in the international for that depend.

Who desires to take the lead in this motion?

I accept as proper with for-income groups need to take the lead. Again, we'll communicate a hint bit more about that after we communicate about the financial approach.

I actually have a CDC, Community Development Corporation, and I find it irresistible. Right now we're revitalizing houses and we're setting marginalized human beings into the ones homes, and I love that.

Remember, non-profits are constantly searching out tactics to fund subjects. I virtually have a for-profits, I anticipate that for-income commercial enterprise owners want to take the lead. They recognize how to reveal a profits. We're able to help urban citizens with jobs. We'll talk extra about some of this later.

That's why a number of you reading this e-book, I apprehend you're available, have the sources, in addition to the economic backing. You can partner with us and without a doubt take this round the area, but beginning collectively with your very personal network.

That's in reality the trouble with the diverse metropolis groups. We have suppressed an environment for enterprise fitness. That's what we're looking for to transport up closer to. We're looking for to improve up marketers simply so we're able to get this transferring ahead.

You're going to need help from your network partners, just like the local government, in order to create the surroundings to have wholesome commercial enterprise entities.

I suppose that's the actual trouble: that for-earnings need to take the lead. That's now not taking area loads in our city groups. We need to get inside the returned of for-profits, our local authorities officials, our religious leaders, and non-income.

We're seeing this paintings right proper here in Toledo. Sustainable Local Foods is a for-income commercial company agency that's looking to make a income, that's looking for to placed forth low price healthy ingredients, and it's miles jogging. They realize how to do that.

What statistics does each accomplice supply to the table?

Everybody is an expert in their own location. Local government has the investment that's to be had. They apprehend the manner to open up financial possibilities that allow some of those items to manifest.

Business proprietors carry the practices and apprehend a manner to positioned systems in location. Again, the internal metropolis keeps us privy to the issues. Everybody has an knowledge, from funding, to skills development, to, in our case, "repurposing houses," to identifying those who can decorate high quality quantities of coins, to folks who understand a way to assist with town farming, to people who recognize a way to help with transportation and packaging.

Everybody brings their individual know-how to the table. You want that. Again, like I said in advance, I didn't recognize whatever approximately farming, or urban farming for that depend extensive variety, but I do understand the way to get with the proper people who are capable of deliver me an training as to how I can make a contribution.

We'll speak about that during detail in a bit bit. Because I clearly have a community improvement agency, I'm capable to accumulate nice homes for basically no longer whatever. People or corporations can make a contribution to a 501 three[c] and get a tax credit score rating.

I companion with Sustainable Local Foods, that is a for-income, and the magic takes location. There are those one-of-a-type partnerships that might take vicinity. We're all experts in some location and we need to deliver that to the desk.

Why is it crucial to get to recognise neighborhood organizations in urban neighborhoods?

That's so crucial. I'm satisfied you asked that query. Each community has a exquisite time desk. Where I pastor, the pals are worried about protection and safety. We'll talk about this whilst we get to what we're doing in terms of the "massive idea" as it pertains to scale.

Right now there's a belongings available for us, it's clearly land, wherein we're hoping to elevate up an energy inexperienced greenhouse shape. It's in the network. It is some blocks down from our church, in an urban surroundings.

I needed to meet with that unique network organisation to allow them to apprehend what we're trying to do. I knowledgeable them that we'll be generating healthy substances and developing jobs. They needed to recognize that so it wouldn't get of their manner or disrupt their trouble of safety.

They have been happy that I known as them. They stated, "Dr. James thank you for calling us. We had been wondering what have emerge as going to expose as plenty as that belongings, because it was as soon as one of the Toledo Public Schools, however they tore that down."

We met with TPS, Toledo Public Schools, and knowledgeable them what we're doing, and that they were enthusiastic about allowing us to apply that belongings. If I didn't meet with that network corporation, they may have felt that I disrespected them.

I located out that there are protection issues, protecting our pals and our homes. At the end of the day, additionally they realise that a part of their time table is to provide jobs and opportunities for human beings, so there was a fit.

I legit them. It surely says I understand your agenda, and it's essential that every one of you find that out, because of the reality every neighborhood group has a excellent time desk. You want to return along and tell them how you can help with healthy components.

Every network is incredible. However, I experience you could earn a effective reaction via virtually attaining out.

Why is it crucial to sell possession in city renewal?

Again, ownership ties in with the entire scalability piece. Right now, I won't care an excessive amount of approximately Microsoft, however if I had been to shop for inventory, I is probably tracking Microsoft each day to ensure they're a success. Right now I don't count on too much approximately Toyota cars, but if I changed into to buy stock in Toyota vehicles, then I'm going to look out for what's taking place with the corporation every and every day.

I teach in my church that Jesus said, "Wherever your coronary coronary heart is, that's wherein your treasures are going to be." I tell the people I pastor, "Wherever you want your coronary coronary heart to be, that's in which you want to position your cash. Whatever you adore, you're going to useful resource it together collectively along with your time and collectively with your cash."

I don't care what humans say they love. I can inform what you like via way of searching at the way you spend a while and your checkbook stubs. That's simply the lowest line.

If we inspire possession and encourage human beings to take a look at the larger picture thru pronouncing that, we're satisfied you're part of transportation and we're glad which you're helping us and studying approximately seeding and planting, and we're happy which you're helping inside the administrative place of job as we bring together this city farming infrastructure.

But if I see your faithfulness and spot that you're devoted, and I say to you…"You're seeing this all spherical you, and ultimately you could personal your non-public meals growing unit. You may be capable of make a notable income, and we're capable of make that take region for you." This goes to hold you in the game.

That's going to encourage you. You're going to get this imaginative and prescient that you're now not simplest a worker, but there's a manner that lets in you to flow into up the ladder. There's a way that you will be promoted to proudly owning your private company in town farming.

To me, that creates extra of an thrilling perception, in desire to certainly an man or woman going to artwork each day doing a little factor in transportation or packaging. That's super, making some respectable coins, however you could expect me lengthy-term, due to the fact I even have a imaginative and prescient of proudly owning my very personal business company sooner or later.

That is what we're looking for to create. That's plan B of this entire operation.

What does the term "We are better together" propose?

That's one of the phrases I say at my church. It's a word that I as soon as heard Rick Warren say. Think about it, we're higher collectively. Within the context of the church, I say we worship higher together.

I tell the people that I pastor that you could worship thru the usage of yourself, however you may't fellowship with the useful resource of yourself. I tell humans, the church isn't always really an area you move, as an opportunity it's a family to which you belong.

You have a herbal own family, but you actually have a religious own family. Within the context of this bankruptcy of making a community of companions, we really are better together.

Everybody brings their facts, they carry their belief, they create their passions, and they create their power. When we come collectively, we're higher together. We get more subjects executed together. We're higher collectively.

Together, we will float mountains. Think approximately it. In any stroll of life, whilst you're taking walks with people who've the same passion which you have, ahead thinkers, in case you bring your strength, your vision, your exhilaration, and your goals together, then you definately definately in reality are better collectively.

I'm for the reason that show up now, no longer remarkable in the church worldwide, however even inside the business organisation international as we're looking for to create an surroundings of productivity.

How will we recognize if the motion is bringing about renewal?

You're going to deliver fruit. There's a criterion. Right now after eight months of starting this movement, one of the matters we're doing is providing jobs. That's an indicator that the motion is transferring beforehand.

We have purchasers who are continuously searching for our meals. That's a sign that we're being successful. We're producing wholesome meals and we're doling out healthful substances.

People are playing our food. They're pronouncing it's even better than natural. They love the flavor.

I suppose that's a sign. We're exposing human beings to metropolis farming. We have younger humans, working young adults, who're starting to see that there's an opportunity profession path if they so choose.

We're creating a buzz in our network. We're displaying that you could carry humans together. You can deliver organizations together, and not just speak about renewal, however really make some matters arise.

We're seeing this display up inside the short-term. You need to have a few results. I've been announcing it time and again on this interview that if we will create jobs and create monetary possibilities, we can say that's a terrific day. At the forestall of the day, we are able to say we've been productive.

How are we able to benefit momentum?

You need to get in and do it. Momentum comes from bringing people collectively. Momentum comes from stepping out of doors the field.

Momentum comes from this e-book that I prepare.

I became telling the satisfactory oldsters at Sustainable Local Foods that this is some issue we want to get out to the region. This is something I've been enthusiastic about for years, no longer handiest developing a spiritual impact, but moreover making an existential effect.

Momentum says, I'm going to take a weekend and placed a majority of those mind together and write a book, and that's exactly what I've finished. You have to shake some subjects up. You've had been given to step out of doors the ordinary conversations of humans talking about exchange and make it take area.

Momentum is at the same time as you repurpose a building and located a food growing unit in for human beings to appearance. That's what I love approximately the parents at Sustainable Local Foods. By the way, you can visit SustainableLocalFoods.Com and see a number of the matters we've finished. Also, you can touch me at William.James@SustainableLocalFoods.Com.

We placed pores and pores and skin in the sport. We in reality are developing food proper now. We have a first rate environment. I'd love an amazing way to return to Toledo, Ohio and be aware what we're doing.

Movement comes from movement. You need to pass. You need to make topics appear, and that's what we're doing right here.

How do you add more community partners?

Along the way, we're for the cause that this motion has a lifestyles of its non-public. You can carry your public colleges to the desk. We're speakme to hospitals. Think approximately all of the humans that hospitals ought to feed. They see the capability here.

You want to begin bringing seniors into the partnership. When you're a senior, you're with a piece of success in search of to consume better. Therefore, via the use of the seniors being a part of this wholesome meals initiative, they may be protected as an anchor organization.

I'm genuinely offering you with some examples of community leaders: organisation owners, religious leaders, and authorities. They can get the ball rolling, however you could add entities and people along the manner.

It starts to take a life of its very personal. I'm appreciating the communicate we're having right now with Toledo Public Schools, the nearby hospitals proper right here, and with a number of the senior citizen corporations. They say, "We love what you're doing and we need to be part of it."

You truely add along the way. We can talk greater approximately that at the same time as you get to that segment. Please contact me for similarly dialogue.

What can damage the motion?

Selfishness. There's the capability to make lots of money and I apprehend that's going to be the attractive factor for industrial business organization proprietors. That's why we're searching for to lure coronary coronary coronary heart-targeted commercial enterprise people.

We recognise that for most corporation proprietors the bottom line is profits. That's why I'm satisfied that the organization proprietors and for-profits are taking the lead. When I say coronary coronary coronary heart-minded, we're talking about individuals who not nice want to expose a income, but they're worried about human beings and planet as well.

When you've got were given those sorts of humans onboard, you apprehend it's not a egocentric component, if it's quite lots being worthwhile then sooner or later this momentum will die out.

For company owners who're analyzing this ebook, there may be instances on the identical time as you aren't growing a income, as an possibility you're paying your humans and seeking to live afloat. You have to preserve that during mind. It's now not the profits that's going to maintain this sustainable. You should make an entire lot of money, but there wants to be a more motivation.

The greater motivation is knowing that you're helping humans and protective the planet that God has given us and that we're being specific stewards of this planet. We're all underneath control. I agree with God places positive property in our ownership and we need to be "pinnacle stewards" or correct managers.

God has no longer most effective placed material possessions in our hands, but he's moreover introduced sure human beings inner our lives to assist perform his venture of reconciliation and loving carrier.

If I became to function some other, the "quadruple bottom line" can be motive. That's what continues a movement going. We're no longer individual-pushed. We're cause driven. Thank you, Rick Warren.

That's what this whole movement is prepared. There's a reason to assist humans, to alternate the environment, and to elevate the quantity of humanity. That's important.

What is the number one cause of this movement?

The most crucial recognition of the motion is to help people, to enhance their existence, to renew the town community, and to present people desire.

Again, food opportunities and desire, I suppose, are what human beings need proper now. Hope is especially needed inside the metropolis environment. I stumble upon some of folks that are hopeless and don't see a manner out. It's a vicious cycle of ache, and most humans are in survival mode, really looking to make it every day.

They have greater bills than cash. We desire to help alternate that. That's the inducement, to encourage humans. I bear in mind metropolis farming can try this. You don't ought to simply exist from every day. Most humans are truly present and no longer definitely thriving. I consider that what we're doing can feature human beings from just surviving to thriving.

That's virtually our purpose. Jim Bloom and I are cause-driven guys. We need to honor God in a huge way, that's our motto, and we need to help people in a massive manner. That's what we're doing.

Where do we begin forming this institution?

It starts offevolved offevolved proper wherein you're. It starts offevolved via identifying the gamers in your community. If you want what we're announcing, it starts offevolved with metropolis hydroponics. It begins offevolved offevolved with investigating how that might paintings on your precise community.

I'll tell you proper now, maximum low-earnings town contexts will welcome this approach. That's why we're right right right here: to offer a model that can be duplicated. It starts offevolved offevolved with getting our minds off of really town agriculture and network gardens, which may be amazing efforts, and begin that specialize in subjects at the manner to create sustainability and scalability.

That's why metropolis hydroponics is a place to begin, to clearly test out and study that, in addition to to go back see what we're doing.

Can this partnership be duplicated in unique town contexts?

Absolutely, that's the purpose. A accurate lengthy-term financial approach desires to be each sustainable and scalable. We hold throwing those phrases spherical because of the truth without scalability, it's clearly going to fall to the wayside.

That's the significance of this model. It lets in us at the manner to reproduction. Right now, Detroit, Michigan is right down the road, in reality. Going on seventy five north it's approximately an hour power, and we're already putting in location the plans in Michigan.

We have Michigan buyers who are purchasing for our meals proper now. We're in Toledo, Ohio, and we've already obtained some abandoned Michigan Public Schools. Obviously, Michigan Public Schools are rebuilding, and we're meeting with spiritual leaders there who I comprehend.

We're permitting them to understand our plans and we're going to repurpose those houses. I'm obsessed with repurposing homes in Michigan. We're doing it in Ohio. We can do it in New York. We can do it in Illinois. This may be duplicated anywhere within the usa!

Chapter 10: Discovering Your Economic Strategy

I want to begin this bankruptcy off with a mirrored image question. Was there ever a time whilst helping someone succeed have become greater important than earning earnings?

Absolutely. I grew up in a pastor's home, I'm a PK (pastor's kid), and one of the topics I cherished approximately my father, the late Bishop James, and my mother who is nevertheless with us, the belief that our calling in lifestyles is to assist humans.;

Life is set loving God and loving people. It's about relationships. I watched my parents help the marginalized, oppressed, and the hurting. That modified into installation my DNA early on and I've tried to carry out their undertaking ever because of the reality.

One of the matters that includes thoughts is supporting distinct community pastors. I undergo in thoughts for a three hundred and sixty 5 days or so I advocated my congregation to journey with me even as one-of-a-type pastors might invite me to come lower back and share God's phrase.

Within our precise context, they may beautify an providing for you when you hold forth, after you educate, absolutely to reveal that they respect you. We call it a "love offering." In my coronary coronary heart, I stated I wasn't going to take that. I desired to reveal the affection of God. I wasn't seeking to make any coins.

In reality, we'd take a economic seed over to the church and talk that, "We're right here to love on you. We're right here to plant a seed. We're right here to sow financially due to the fact we need you to be blessed. We want you to revel in our love, and we're going to do it in a tangible manner, consequently I'm no longer receiving any services."

The pastors were blown away from my act of generosity! Again, in maximum Christian contexts, in case you percentage a phrase or train, if you're a pastor, they favor to enhance you "a love imparting", as we name it, however I refused.

You may additionally additionally ask, what is the price of this? There are such loads of factors we're capable of talk about. I can see that our church has been blessed because of those efforts. I completed these acts of kindness for a 12 months. I cherished being able to pass and sow into a few different church, another pastor, and their dream. I wasn't seeking out any form of go lower back, besides the move returned of showing love.

The Bible says, "Owe no man some detail but love." There's a few difficulty satisfying about that.

Please provide an explanation for your model for economic possibility: food, opportunity, and choice.

That's in fact the subtitle of my e-book, and that's what it's approximately. We're supplying healthy meals. Think about the benefits right here. That's going to assist people experience higher and look higher. We all need that. We're providing opportunities. We're going to talk about repurposing homes.

We can repurpose empty loads. While we're repurposing homes, we also can create jobs. Then the desire element is the dimensions, where we're capable of installation strength green greenhouse systems round the arena, similarly to enhance up entrepreneurship.

That's in truth our model: food, possibilities and preference. That gives the vision of what we're trying to find to do. There's hundreds within the ones 3 terms. You can see that I'm unpacking those terms on this e-book.

How lots cash is being spent in Toledo metro within "50 miles" on exporting end result and greens internal a calendar 365 days?

I count on that's the amazing part. The enterprise owners are going to go back alive on this element. When you are announcing Toledo metro, you're definitely speaking inside a 50 mile radius of Toledo.

According to a USDA 2009 test the common character in Toledo, Ohio, or interior 50 miles, devour 1.Three cups of fruit constant with day or 188 kilos in step with 12 months.

Also, in keeping with a USDA 2009 have a look at, the commonplace Toledoan consumes 1.Fifty 8 cups of vegetables an afternoon or 28lbs consistent with yr.

The USDA advocated quantity is two.6 cups of veggies an afternoon, or 475lbs consistent with 12 months. I need you to notice that with each stop end result and veggies, the advocated amount is a lot extra. The overall vegetable intake is 270,371,696lbs yearly at $2.00 common in line with pound. The typical produce intake is 446,781,692lbs at $2.00 commonplace in line with pound.

In specific phrases, the market ability at current intake is $893,563,384 bucks, Wow!

Are you ready for your minds to be blown? Based on the USDA recommended consumption of each quit stop result and vegetables, the marketplace capability is a whopping $1,538,123,412!

Please allow me to increase your commercial enterprise organization potential with a few more case research. Not simplest are we presently establishing SLF in Toledo, however additionally in Columbus, Ohio and Detroit, Michigan as well.

In Columbus Metro, the marketplace capability at modern consumption for each end result and greens at $2.00 common steady with pound is

$2,497,637,688. In Ohio, there are 11,536,504 residents consistent with 2010 census.

Please understand that inside the State of Ohio, the entire capability modern-day-day sales at $2.00 commonplace in line with lb. Is $10,982,751,808!

The USDA recommended consumption income at $2.00 commonplace in step with lb. Is $18,873,720,544. Folks, these numbers are fantastic! But those offer every information and forecasts for the State of Ohio.

By now, you're in all likelihood jumping up and down as you can see the capability for you and your town.

If you watched those numbers can also offer you with a functionality coronary coronary heart attack, permit me allow you to understand approximately Michigan. In Michigan Metro, at $2.00 not unusual in step with lb. The marketplace capability at present day intake is $3,829,227,696.

Based at the USDA advocated intake, the marketplace functionality is $6,576,479,488. These ability numbers may be more or lots less on your specific community. Nevertheless, this industrial organization possibility is unmatched with the resource of maximum.

I advocate, wherein else can you are making insane portions of money and really help human beings at the same time?

Let me offer you with the method to help you to decide your marketplace capability. Please don't forget that the marketplace capability in any given region may be determined through taking the in keeping with capita consumption instances the populace within the preferred marketplace area.

The ensuing determine represents the overall market. Studies show that it's far less expensive to count on to benefit at minimum a 5%, marketplace percentage and as immoderate as 25% with a advanced fantastic product over the competition.

It is our goal at SLF to capture 2% of the Toledo nearby marketplace by using the usage of 12 months five, 5 % by way of the usage of three hundred and sixty five days 7, and 10% by means of of the use of way of twelve months 10.

To accomplish this we are able to need to put into impact our "three year plan," and to accomplice with capacity clients who will help. For information at the facts of this three three hundred and sixty five days plan, e mail me at: William.James@Sustainablefoods.Com.

What is the distinction among the "triple backside line" version rather than the single backside line model?

I've alluded to it in advance than, however now that we're on this bankruptcy approximately discovering your financial method, for maximum organisation owners the lowest line is earnings.

When we talk approximately the triple backside line, it's now not surely profit, but humans, planet and reason. While the others interest on one element, we cognizance on all 3.

What are social entrepreneurs?

The social marketers are the ones people or companies of people that come together and create answers to a number of the huge social desires.

I hold in thoughts myself a "pastorpreneur," but I'm possibly moreover a social entrepreneur. They want to make matters take area on a large scale. That's what we're looking to do.

As a pastorpreneur, I want to enhance not handiest the fitness of my church, however additionally the fitness of our surrounding surroundings.

I love social entrepreneurs because of the fact they're continuously deliberating big solutions for massive issues on a massive scale. That's what they do.

How does growing nearby produce provide jobs?

Again, it's the location of wherein we're developing factors. We're preserving it inside the town network due to the fact we apprehend that's where renewal takes location. We're putting in remarkable places, during our city, in which we're installing those developing devices.

For every vicinity wherein we installation a developing unit, we need employees. As I said in advance, every half of of acre of developing area requires 167 hours of labor every week, because of this we need to hire people to try this. That's what we're seeing occurring.

The extra growing devices, the more jobs.

What is the difference the diverse vintage monetary version versus the new edition that you are setting into action?

Again, I recognise town planners and social activists were reviewing special fashions for pretty a while. Professor Michael Porter at Harvard has finished a extremely good activity in his artwork on "the competitive benefit" in the internal town.

Most of my belief comes from Dr. Porter's document. Generally speaking, the vintage version is a social model. The new version is the "economic version." The antique model is ready redistributing wealth in maximum of the inner metropolis and urban agencies. We're not in fact developing a dwelling or growing wealth.

The authorities's hobby is sincerely to assist and act as a "brief repair," to some thing from vouchers to meals stamps. Ninety-Nine Thousand citizens right here in Toledo, Ohio are food stamp recipients.

There's charity and there's rescue. It's a brief-term, quick repair. The social version is utilized in most metropolis agencies, so the neighborhood government acts as a bandage. A lot of what's going on in the social model is isolation from the bigger network.

What I mean with the aid of that is we're not simply thinking about scalability outside our cities. Again, close by authorities gives maximum of our metropolis commercial enterprise and serves the local people. We're now not actually building bridges in the direction of corporations wherein we must do business organization with outdoor the network.

Many of our professional and skilled minorities who have exceptional stories are high-quality engaged within the social provider region. The government is worried at once in supplying services or funding. That's remarkable. We want that, and that's why we want to deliver them to the desk.

There's this dependence on the close by authorities and social offerings. I anticipate people aren't sincerely asking for a handout. At the surrender of the day, the city network is asking for a hand-up.

There are folks who do want help, and we want to provide that. There are people who do want assist and they do want the short recovery, but it doesn't offer the lengthy-term solution. We want an monetary version that is sustainable.

We want the "personal sector" to step in and offer a for-profits agency like what we're doing with Sustainable Local Foods. We want companies which is probably export-orientated. We need agencies that may think out of doors of the network.

As I stated earlier, we need the authorities. That's why I need community government on my group and for your company. Let's interest on improving the environment for corporations.

With this economic model, we are able to function town environments to empower entrepreneurs and to create a sustainable version. We want to make this shift from the vintage version, this is a social redistribution of the wealth, to the economic model, that is being worthwhile, possibilities, and lengthy-time period answers.

That's what we're doing right here.

Can you provide a case look at of an gift food version powered via hydroponics?

Yes, Cleveland Green City Growers, who also are located in Ohio. You can appearance them up at the internet. They have an first rate greenhouse that they started from scratch. It's captivating. It sits on 3 acres of land.

I anticipate the clinic and some wonderful community businesses helped to build it. They're developing lettuce proper now, and the lettuce goes to place ingesting locations and shops.

Green City Growers is simply one of the maximum vital food production greenhouses in any given metropolis place. I count on what they're doing is remarkable. The horrible is they spent tens of loads of lots of greenbacks, to gather this greenhouse from scratch. It bleeds a whole lot of electricity, and it is able to't be duplicated throughout the us of a. We can turn this proper right into a powerful, via constructing a fee-effective, electricity green greenhouse shape that doesn't bleed pretty a few strength. The one in Cleveland does. We need with a view to take it for the duration of the u . S ..

Again, I apprehend urban planners and social activists have been reviewing exclusive fashions for quite some time.

Even even though there's the tremendous of the Cleveland Green City Growers and they're doing a little awesome things there, I assume it's too high priced, and it's not power efficient. I should argue that we need to move towards a fee-effective model, as well as an strength inexperienced model, that we are capable of take throughout the area.

We'll preserve you published on our development! Just go to our internet site www.SustainableLocalFoods.Com or depart a message at William.James@SustainableLocalFoods.Com and we'll pass from there.

Based on what you've got were given have been given said about the amount of cash being spent on importing forestall result and greens, why is it important to enhance the close by growing market, specially inside the urban community?

Basically, we're giving our coins away! We're redistributing wealth. We're not genuinely creating it. When it involves purchasing for give up result and vegetables from outdoor, we're paying coins to get it proper proper here, we're paying taxes, and we're paying freight fees.

Why not produce wholesome meals property locally? That's what we're looking for to do in Toledo. Again, in case you reflect onconsideration on it, most of what we produce right here in Toledo, ninety eight percent of the produce consumed with the beneficial aid of Toledoans comes from over 1,800 miles away.

All we're pronouncing is, do it regionally. We're preventing for the close by presence. We can create wealth proper right here. We're telling the opportunity folks who are growing regionally, which isn't always lots, to maintain what you do, genuinely don't buy from outdoor of our network.

With this 24-hour food production internet site, we will create wealth, and we can hold the cash in our network.

Why should for-earnings groups, now not non-income, take the lead in city renewal?

Most non-income are restricted by manner of funding and that would lessen renewal efforts.

Nonprofits rely on one-of-a-kind entities for financial help. On the opposite hand, for-earnings exist to make a income. Basically, they have got structures in place which might be designed to deliver a excessive first-rate coins float.

Why is it crucial that the close by government help decorate the surroundings for community company improvement?

Sometimes the government can get inside the manner of that. Sometimes the government turns into a bandage and they're now not truly helping nearby agencies. Sometimes they're taxed to loss of life.

We need to create an environment that allows them to thrive. I like what's occurring right right here in Toledo due to the fact our new economic director is making an attempt to do this.

If small agencies can thrive with out all the crimson tape, then we can get once more to what this u.S. Changed into built upon, small companies, and create jobs. I take delivery of as proper with we want to recapture that entrepreneurial spirit in our metropolis monetary environment.

The network government has the strength to try this.

How can a non-earnings accomplice with a nearby authorities to consistent fee variety for monetary development?

That's the splendor of a non-profit. Most towns have their community Port Authority. We have the Toledo Port Authority, and that they have what you name the CEDI. These are Community Economic Development Initiative bucks which is probably most effective given to non-income.

My non-earnings is able to collect $35,000 in provide cash to do monetary improvement art work in underserved organizations. I stated in advance that we're looking to assemble an strength green greenhouse form.

The problem with most greenhouses is that they bleed plenty of electricity. We're capable of get predevelopment budget that allow us to have a take a look at what at the way to seem like proper now. We are currently doing predevelopment artwork on a capability greenhouse model.

Those price range aren't available to apply inside the path of for-income corporations. I may encourage industrial company proprietors to create their non-public non-earnings, or companion with one, and discover the opportunities.

In the case of what we're doing in our partnership with Sustainable Local Foods is we're capable of acquire residences, in maximum instances donated, due to the reality we're a non-earnings.

We have a neighborhood land financial group right right here, and you may have a few element like that. They're self sufficient, but its authorities related. They collect homes which have gone into foreclosures, and essentially as a non-income, we can gather the ones homes for, definitely, pennies on the dollar.

Some of these houses that we accumulate are able to be repurposed. As a non-earnings, we gather the houses. The for-profits, in this example, Sustainable Local Foods, places the developing gadgets in the property, and my non-earnings collects the lease. That's one way of having a productive partnership.

Please describe the importance of a for-earnings commercial enterprise partnering with some specific for-earnings for monetary renewal.

That's a lovable state of affairs as properly, because of the truth no longer best do I actually have a non-earnings that allows city citizens, I even have a for-profits entity, in which we act as a well-known contractor.

What's really neat about this is, I don't need to understand hundreds approximately protection, janitorial, painting, demolition, or garden care, but we've were given contracts contemporary with the town wherein we're capable of do all of the ones matters.

What I do is, "sub-settlement" out the work. In the case of this wholesome food initiative, my for-income has the workers already in vicinity that could skip in and do the important paintings to ensure the ones homes are in specific situation to repurpose at the internal as we assemble the infrastructure.

Is there a quadruple backside line this is going beyond the triple backside line? Why is Sustainable Local Foods a remarkable method for city renewal?

I touched on that earlier. To me, the fourth bottom line might be strolling in the direction of the motive of owning your personal food growing corporation. In this specific case, the manufacturing of wholesome meals isn't always simply authentic for our our our bodies and our best outlook, but it affords an possibility wherein interior an metropolis farm placing, we're raising up metropolis entrepreneurs.

I'm obsessed on raising up the following era of city farmers. But you want an infrastructure to help produce wholesome food. We're no longer without a doubt generating healthy food, however we're growing an infrastructure as properly.

You need packaging and transportation. It's vital to train people the way to plant with the right water combination. All of this presents to challenge creation. I assume that's the magic on the internal, that town gardening isn't always quite a good deal healthful factors, however it opens the door to lengthy-time period jobs and lengthy-term monetary possibilities.

I apprehend we maintain announcing this time and again once more, but that's the significance of an remarkable commercial enterprise version. It has to offer sustainability and scalability.

How may you define an financial approach?

Here's a quick model: An monetary method has to offer possibility, and it has to provide possibility for truly everybody. It ought to be all-inclusive.

That way, because it relates to jobs, it has to offer opportunities no longer first-class for top notch forms of humans. What I love about what we're doing with this particular economic model is, you can be an ex-culprit or you'll be a veteran, and however make a splendid living as an metropolis farmer.

One will have a immoderate college degree or not, and nevertheless help with planting and transportation. There's an area for each person. It isn't an fantastic financial model if it doesn't provide an opportunity for all.

Chapter 11: The Power of the Local Work Force

What are the roles which can be available in town farming?

We can provide jobs in packaging, transportation, developing, manage, answering telephones, and protection. Those are the sort of things that we can provide lengthy-term, as we build an urban farming infrastructure.

What must be the beginning pay?

We are paying over minimum profits. We're paying our human beings $eleven.00 an hour, that is thrilling. As they preserve growing, we plan on such as to that.

Can human beings or families personal their personal developing gadgets?

That's segment 2 of this, and that's why you need to hold to stay in touch with me. That's what we plan on doing. We're searching at techniques to provide financing in order for capability agency proprietors.

Because we're able to sell the meals on the again prevent, that kind of enterprise version can be paid off interior 4 or 5 years. That's the thrilling element: entrepreneurship. That's what continues the community developing.

How an entire lot can an character earn from proudly owning their very very own developing unit?

Right now we're searching at paying an character or a family $60,000 a three hundred and sixty five days. Can you do not forget? People who've determined on this as a career path also can start out in transportation, safety, or management, and after some years they're making $60,000 a year. The $60,000 is with surely one developing unit.

Imagine growing gadgets or three developing gadgets. We have veterans and ex-offenders who can't locate proper jobs. Now proper here's a possibility and opportunity for the ones citizens to get employment and grow to be marketers. Currently, we're operating with a jail which will introduce this technique of developing meals. This lets in us to repurpose unused location, similarly to, teach the ones inmates who will rapid reenter society.

This is thrilling to me. Let's be real, some humans inside the city groups, are growing marijuana as an entrepreneur in every other industry and that's now not top. .

My component is, some of those humans understand the way to amplify stuff. They apprehend a way to increase flora. Let's do it legally. Let's make it efficient. Now they may be happy with being metropolis farmers with their very very very own growing devices and making $60,000 or greater a one year, legally.

Again, that's the capacity for surely one developing unit. Imagine two, 3, or four. I'm excited about this entire manner.

You touched on this earlier, does one want to have a excessive faculty degree or university degree to achieve success in city farming?

Some of the era is immoderate-effect, so of route a diploma is probably extraordinary. But you do not should have a degree, however, you have to be inclined to research a current approach and be willing to research.

If you don't want to research it is going to be hard, however most people need to beautify their lives. You'd be surprised what I'm seeing in the city businesses. When we create jobs within the community, the loyalty we're seeing from city residents is splendid.

Why is it critical to vicinity those gadget opportunities in areas in which human beings have accessibility?

A lot of humans need to paintings, but they don't have a automobile. They can't get spherical. Why need to they be denied get right of entry to to an great technique? We make sure it's at an area where they will be capable of seize a bus or a place wherein they'll stroll to art work inner a pair blocks.

How masses does it fee for a potential entrepreneur to private a developing unit?

We're looking at that proper now. That's segment 2. You likely want to be part of my mastermind institution, my agency schooling session, so you can check extra about that. We're putting the information together for the cloth as we speak.

Again, that's section 2. I assume we'll be capable of finance the devices due to the fact the payoff on the once more prevent is so brief. We're able to sell the food for you, which would possibly pay off the unit internal four or 5 years.

Because we're able to sell the meals speedy at the returned quit, we have already got those humans in region. We assume that the financing won't be that tough.

To whom do you promote the produce?

We promote to farmers. We're selling to farmer's markets. We have health food shops that buy meals from us. To permit you to realise the reality, that hasn't even been our hassle. It's been quite clean on the way to promote our meals. Our problem is trying to preserve production up with demand! Perhaps, you may associate with me, to help carry out this assignment.

The produce grown proper right here in Toledo is in particular supplied on the Toledo Farmer's Market in downtown Toledo. We're searching out to set up a presence there, and at some special region farmer's markets as properly. We moreover promote food to a few of the close by consuming locations.

What training is needed for metropolis agriculture?

I'm really excited about it due to the truth in April, Alan Halterman joined Sustainable Local Foods agency as a grower. He studied in the town agriculture application at Owens Community College, that could be a university proper right here in Toledo, Ohio. It's unhappy, and masses of had been disillusioned that Owens Community College has stopped presenting the town agricultural software program. The closest locations you can pass in this region are Ohio State or Michigan, however allow's be actual, that's truely too a long way away for human beings to tour.

To train the teenagers in agriculture, Sustainable Local Foods works closely with the Lucas County "Youth Treatment Center," YTC, and the Toledo Juvenile Courts. Many of the younger humans that artwork with us have come from the YTC software. This software program application permits them to acclimate lower back into society similarly to the paintings force.

Our reaction is to create educational programs. Keep in mind, we sincerely started out this about 8 months in the beyond, and it's kind of like having a modern day infant infant, with out going through pregnancy. We're learning alongside the manner.

What we're in search of to do is to create an educational software program program proper right here in Toledo associated with the work that we're doing with the juvenile courts. Again, you don't need a degree to do this, however schooling is important. That's what we're doing.

We're operating with "Toledo Grows," which has opened our eyes to an entire lot of opportunities. They have perception in agriculture, and they do schooling there.

Toledo Grows is also an outreach software program at the Toledo Botanical Gardens that allows with that kind of schooling. Like I said, we're looking at the Lucas County Youth Treatment Center and different nearby programs.

I certainly have an exciting testimony. Medina Robinson is every different considered one of our teens employees. She come to be domestic schooled and just graduated from excessive school. She started out out out education through the teenagers empowerment utility at United North, and started out to artwork proper right here at Sustainable Local Foods tons less than in step with week later.

We interviewed her and he or she or he or he stated, "We plant, feed and harvest city gardens, and it is fun!" She's in truth gambling her revel in proper right here with our younger people.

How does one recruit adults for city farming?

Depending on in which you live, there are one in every of a kind applications. Toledo has an area known as The Source, and it is downtown. Many adults glide there to check genuinely one in every of a kind skills or to determine what their abilties are.

They study interviewing strategies, what it takes to get a challenge, what to wea on an interview, and what their skillset is. They're then placed in a database. Obviously, city farming is something new, but it's our purpose to ensure it's clean to study.

It doesn't take a rocket scientist to discover ways to do city agriculture. We have been taking walks with a community interest finder referred to as The Source, and that they have a database of capability personnel who could probable healthy the entered standards.

Obviously, they do should take a look at some new abilties on this location, but it could be accomplished. There is essentially a chunk pressure already in region in most town corporations. They are ready to head.

How does the city farming network look at with the hard car industry, in particular within the Midwest?

It's up and down. I also can moreover have referred to it in advance, however proper proper here inside the Midwest, some of my factors to whom I pastor have been laid off and they've been in the vehicle enterprise for years. Many of those jobs aren't there. Some have taken early payouts.

I acquire as right with that city gardening will come along and help with that, or ultimately replace the car employer within the Midwest if it maintains to say no. We'll be there as an possibility profession route.

While it has its challenges, by using developing an infrastructure for town farming this, will offer those prolonged-time period hobby opportunities. There are many individuals who ought to skip from the automobile business enterprise and end up urban farmers. It's not attractive, however it's going to pay the payments and you could leave a legacy to the subsequent era.

Describe what an everyday day looks as if within the life of an town farmer.

We're simply at the starting point of it proper right here, however once I walk into the greenhouse, I see people planting. We furthermore have vans out for transportation to supply the meals to a variety of our decrease back give up customers.

We see younger people studying a manner to plant. We have human beings in management. We have media asking for interviews about the hydroponics approach. Like in any regular paintings strain surroundings, there's interest occurring all the time. I envision for the destiny an environment in which humans will come to a sure department of genuinely considered considered one of our establishments and look to shop for their very personal growing unit.

It's some of hobby that focus on wholesome meals manufacturing. On a every day foundation, you may be around this tremendous developing gadget.

What are a number of the benefits and drawbacks of putting in region keep in a greenhouse?

The advantages are that the greenhouses are already in region, you have were given properly temperature, and the environment is proper for growing produce. The downside, yet again, it bleeds quite some strength. That's big.

Right now we're paying lease to Erie Street Market. We're developing a living through way of developing and selling our produce. Our electricity bills were drastically reduced in contrast to the previous vicinity, Oleman's Greenhouse. That's why it's vital to elevate up greenhouse structures that don't bleed that a superb deal strength.

That could be the disadvantage: excessive strength rate. The blessings are which you have already got a commercial organization that's set up and has the critical conditions for developing plants.

Can you perceive or find out a capability artwork pressure in every city context?

You can go online and type in "Work Force," or actually communicate to humans about what you do. A authentic area to start is your neighborhood interest finder or head hunter. You have humans in location who are equipped to artwork.

Many of these groups in spite of the truth that train vital understanding devices, and you could faucet into their database and get the ones sorts of people on your inexperienced industrial business enterprise. It is a privilege to be worried on this technique. Growing healthy meals is wonderful!

Why is it important to offer an possibility profession route for teens graduating from excessive faculty?

Many of them don't need to be docs or prison specialists, or don't enjoy they're clever sufficient or organized to visit college. Some children are simply searching out a assignment after commencement. Urban agriculture can provide an possibility profession course.

The motto can be, "I can increase healthy food, I could make a difference, and I may also need to make some appropriate cash!"

How does one determine the amount of personnel wished in this corporation?

Remember, every half of acre lawn requires three full-time and 3 detail-time people. Obviously, the more developing devices that we installation, the more human beings we're going to hire.

It is our preference that certain human beings or companies of people will subsequently very very own a meals growing business employer. We at SLF are positioning ourselves on the way to finance your "green commercial employer" and educate you a way to grow a green corporation.

Again, if people have the attitude and the selection, an man or woman or own family could run the economic agency and we're capable of sell the produce for them.

Chapter 12: The Plan to Repurpose Existing Buildings

What does it suggest to repurpose a building?

Basically, repurposing is identifying whether or not the constructing has the proper dimensions for the food developing devices. Also, to make certain that the roof is not leaking, that it's no longer beyond repair so we are capable of region a developing unit in there to broaden meals.

How does one find out structures that would service the motive of incorporating a meals developing unit?

What we've finished is we've talked to the close by land monetary institution. The land economic organisation is a part of the close by government. As I stated in advance, they gather homes that have lengthy past into foreclosure for whatever motive. We're now not surely looking at residential homes, however also agency.

Again, each developing unit is ready a half of of-acre. That translates into 35,000-forty,000 square toes or greater. It need to be large enough to house at least one growing unit. That lets in to decide if we are capable of located one in or now not.

What are a few gift structures that could qualify for having a growing unit?

As I said in advance, greenhouses are suited. There are numerous abandoned greenhouses. Many are going out of business corporation for anything motive. I assume that's an extraordinary region to start.

As you have were given have been given referred to earlier, what is the value of working together together with your close by port authority for building a greenhouse?

Here in Toledo, authorities entities similar to the Toledo-Lucas County Port Authority, or perhaps a few other ones wherein you are living, have funding that can sometimes be used for repurposing a constructing because it relates to energy basic performance.

There's money for green initiative efforts. Just check collectively with your network government company. There's additionally coins to assist with power inexperienced duties.

What is the fee of working alongside facet your nearby land economic institution for acquiring homes to repurpose?

I suppose we answered that not straight away. The neighborhood land monetary institution is unbiased. Even even though they're a community authorities organisation, they have got autonomy as properly. They have a few freedom to make faster alternatives. There's typically loads of purple tape almost about the government.

They gather houses on a every day basis. If you sit down down down down with the director of your nearby land monetary organization, you could tell them what you're looking for, and they will help discover a property for pennies at the dollar.

One of the advantages of on foot in town regions is the diverse abandoned systems that can be repurposed. Would you settle?

Yes. That's what we're doing here in Toledo. In reality, the authorities can see in which we're headed. They're part of our community of partners. Some have donated some empty homes for our reason.

www.ingramcontent.com/pod-product-compliance
Lightning Source LLC
Chambersburg PA
CBHW071341120626
46546CB00002B/650